The photo journal
Villach

Matthew Slater

"This heart of mine was made to travel this world"

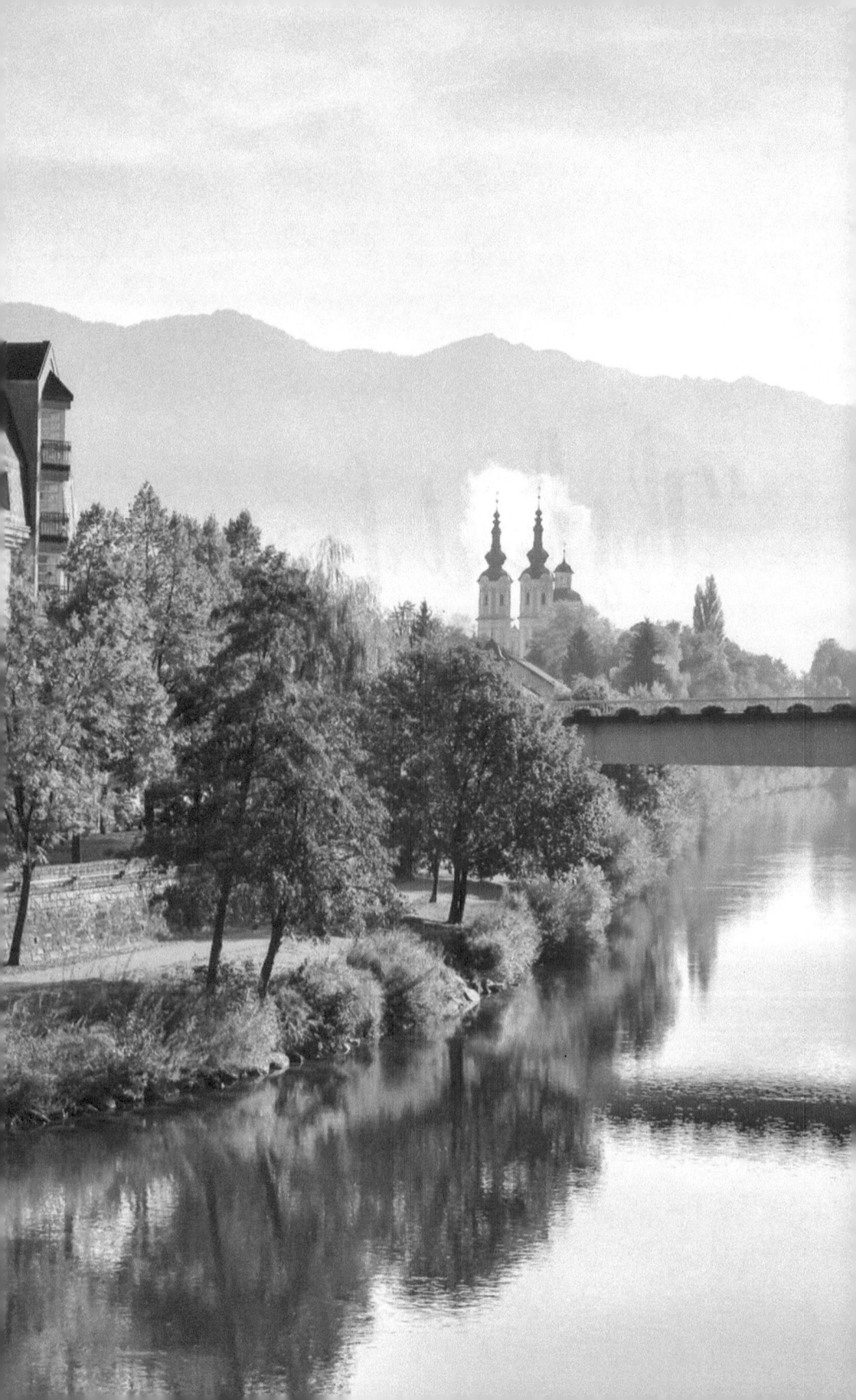

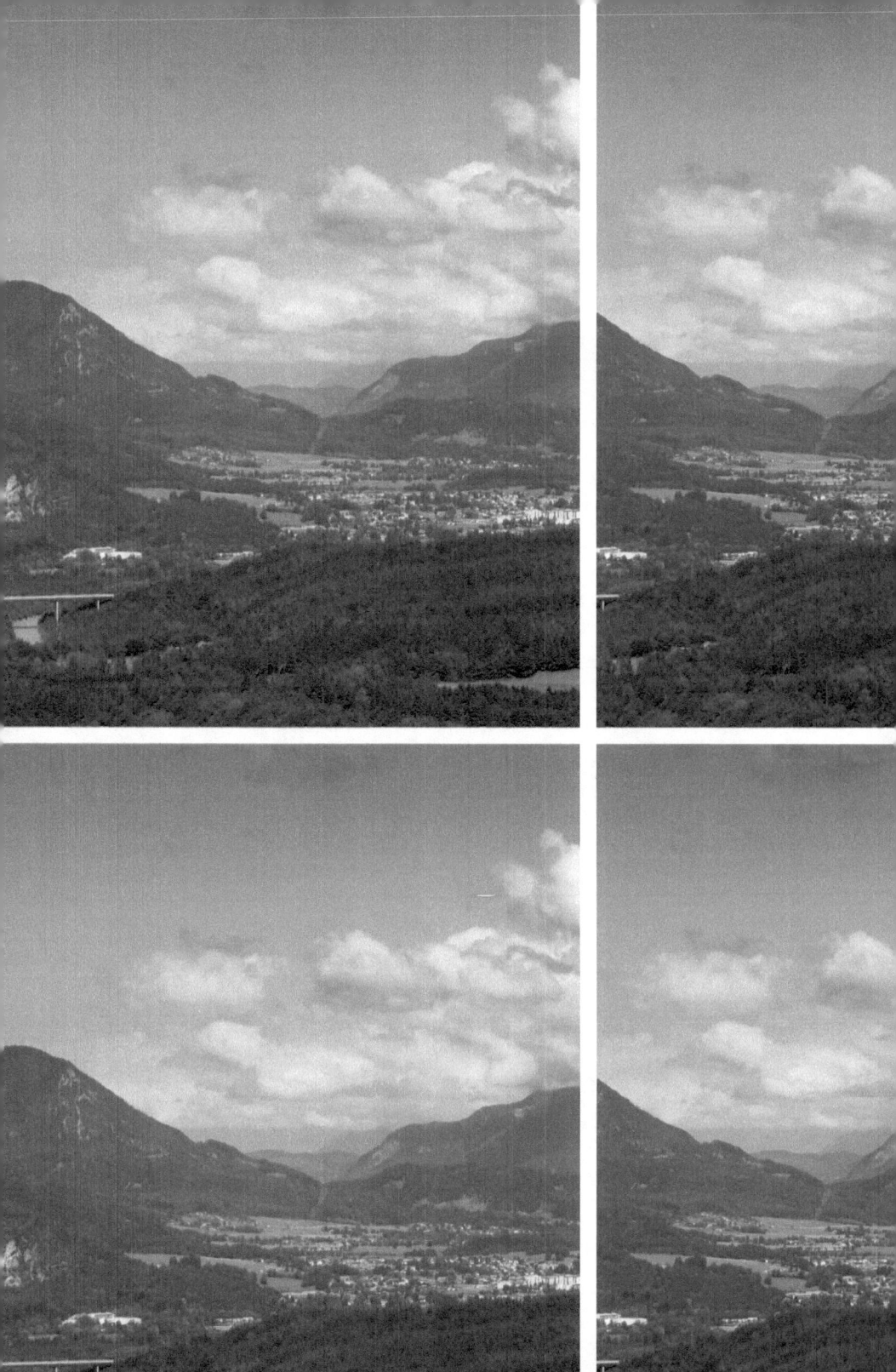

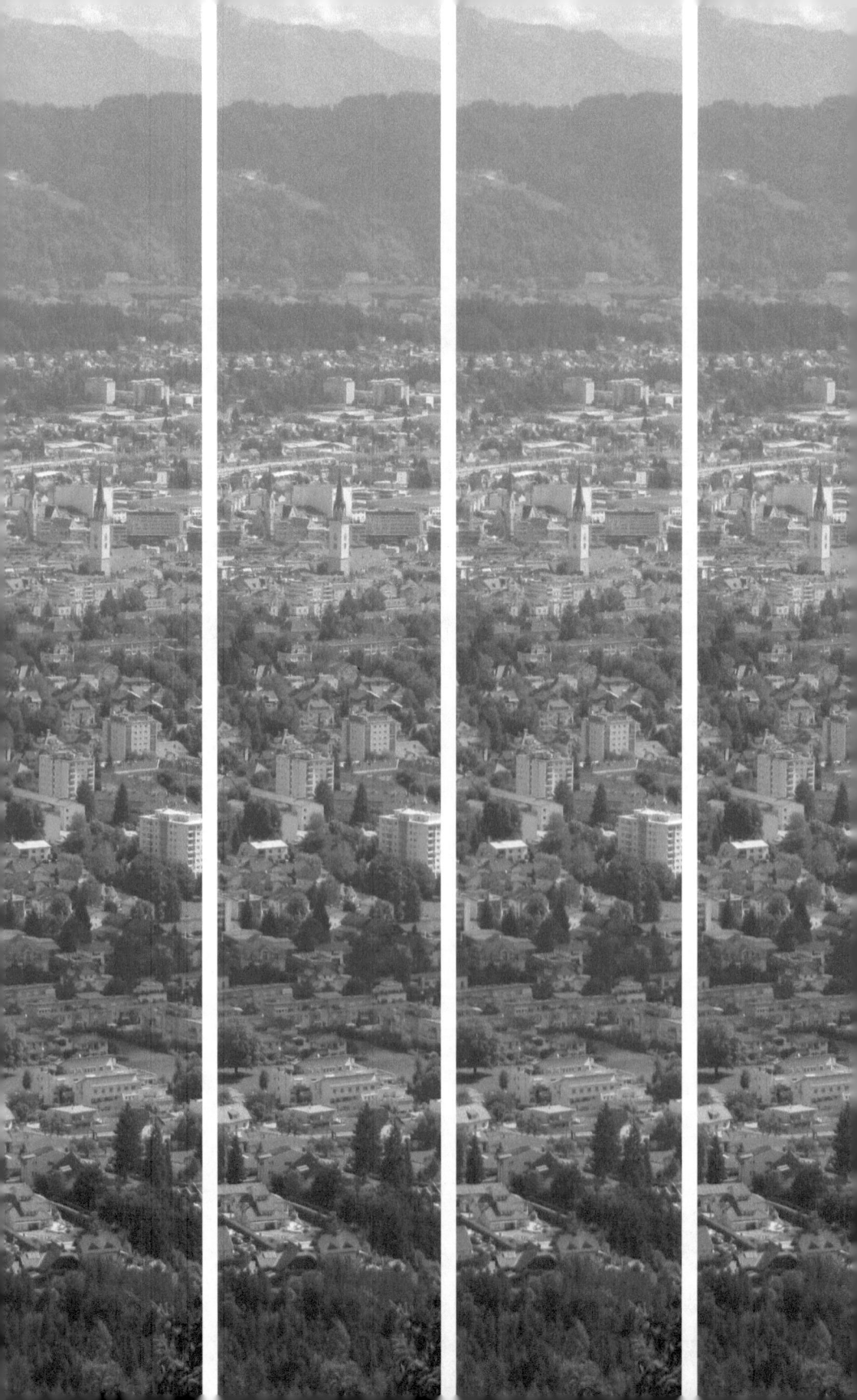

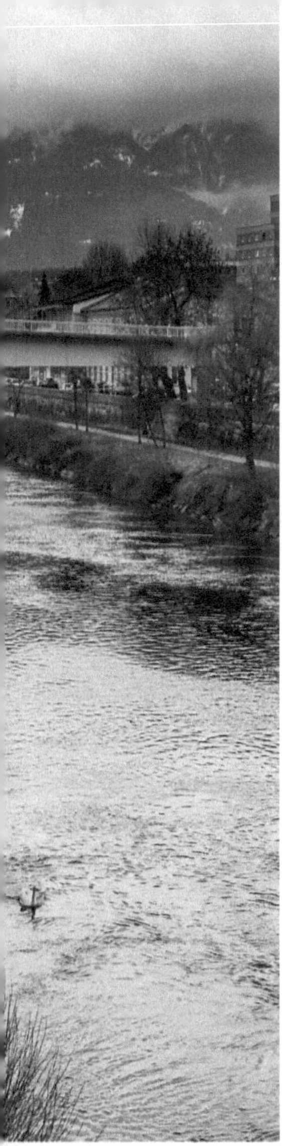

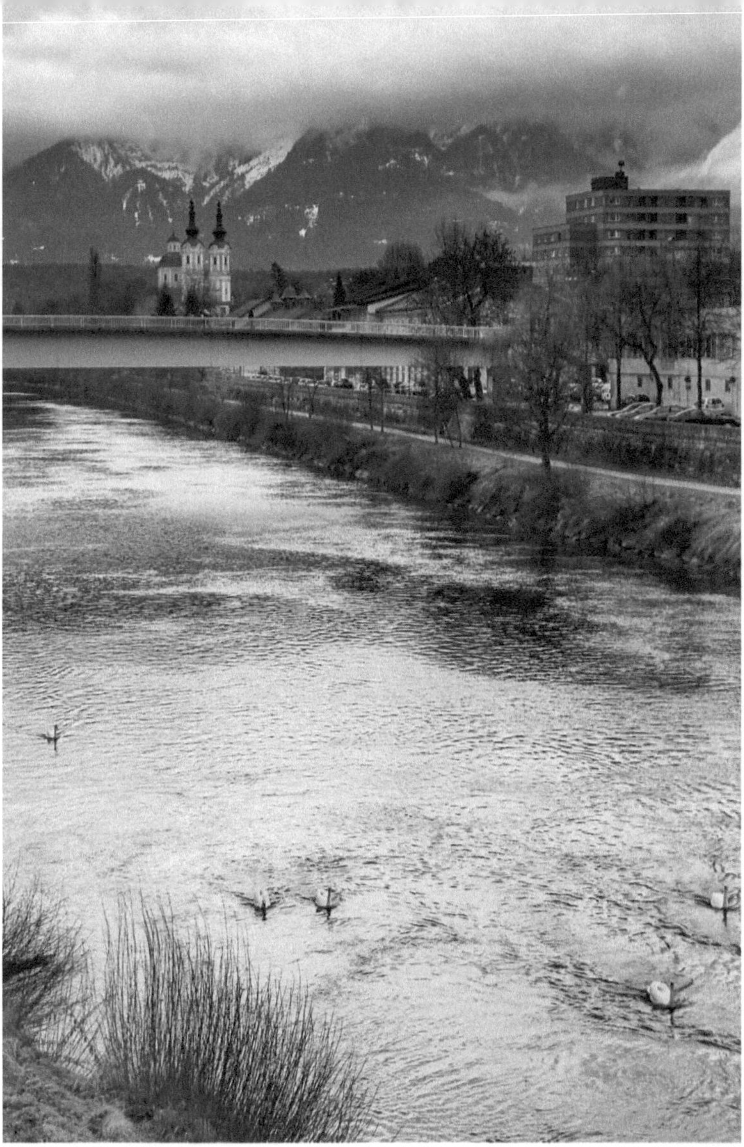

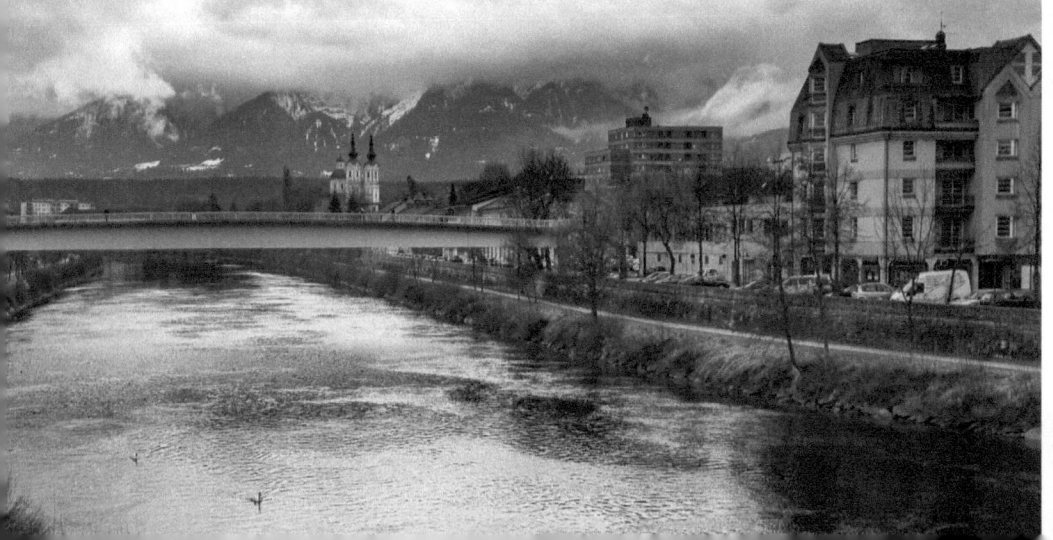

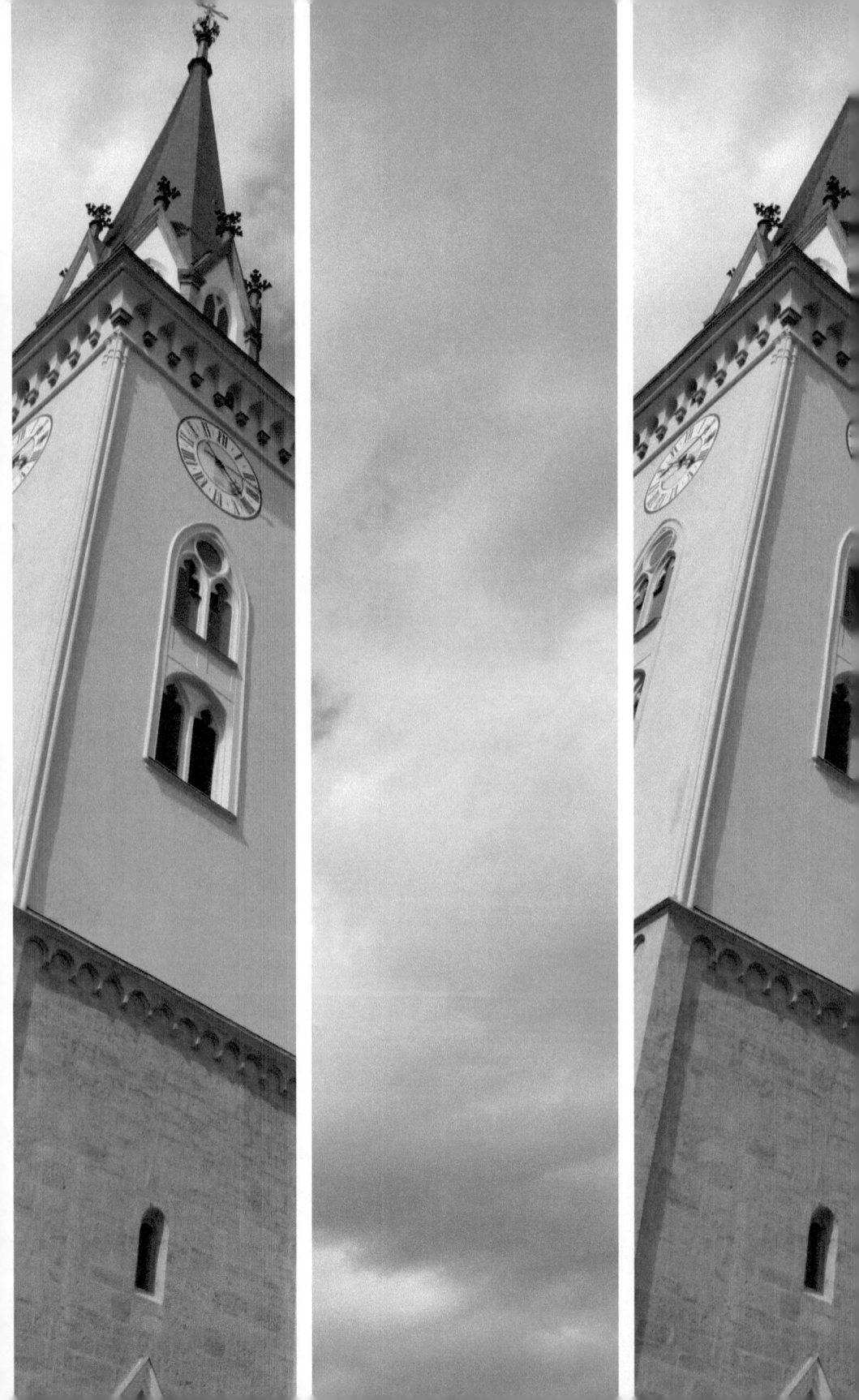

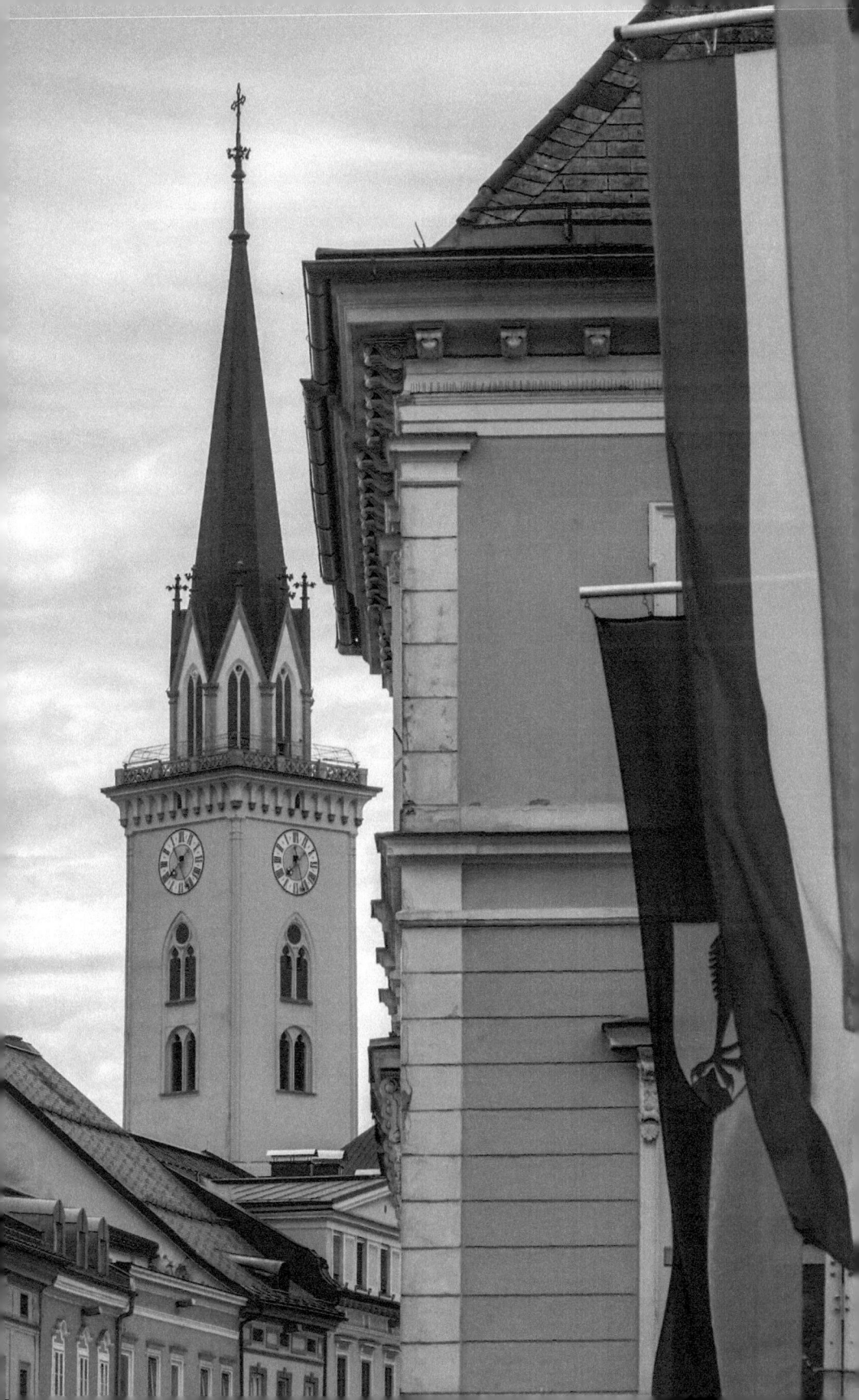

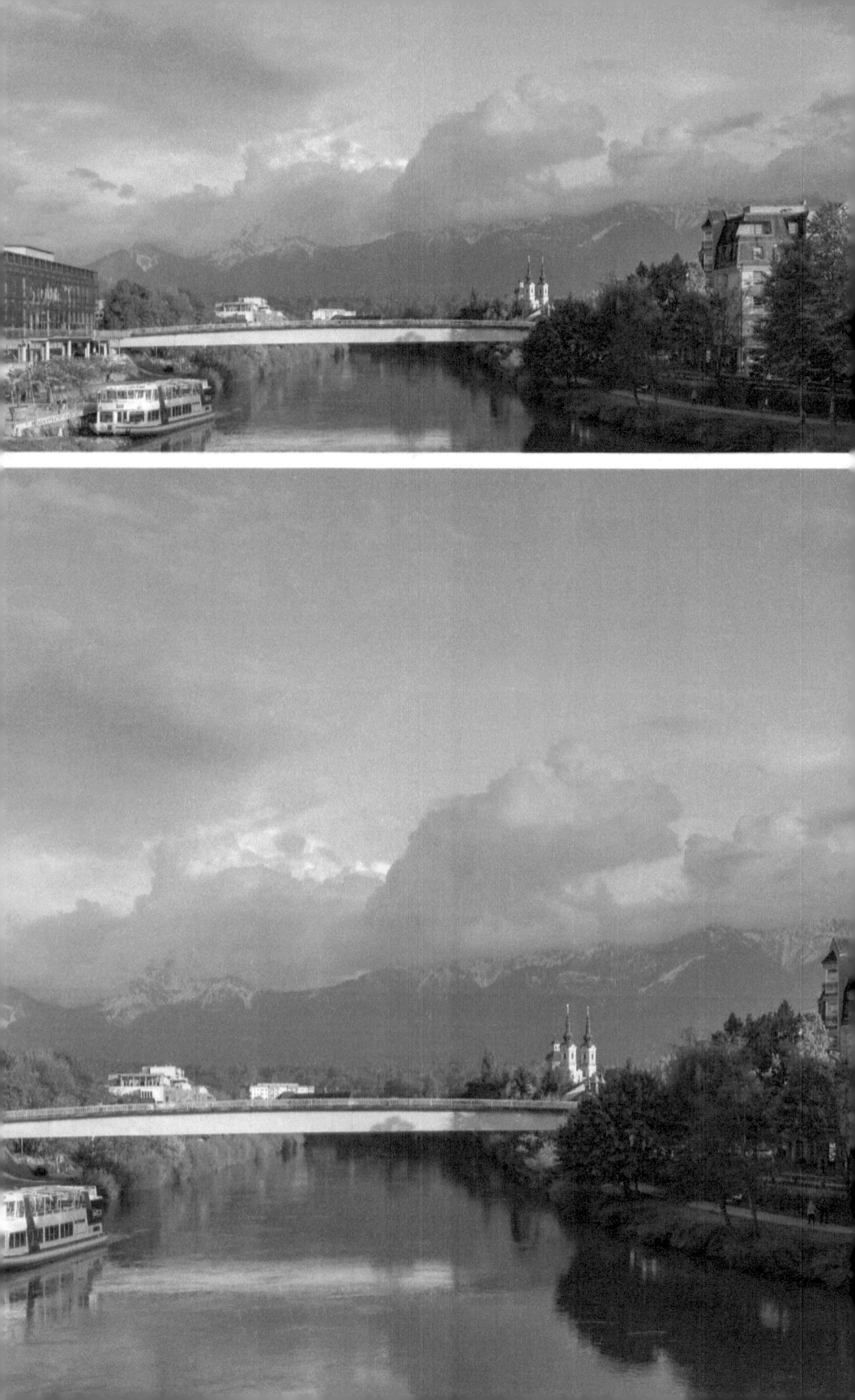

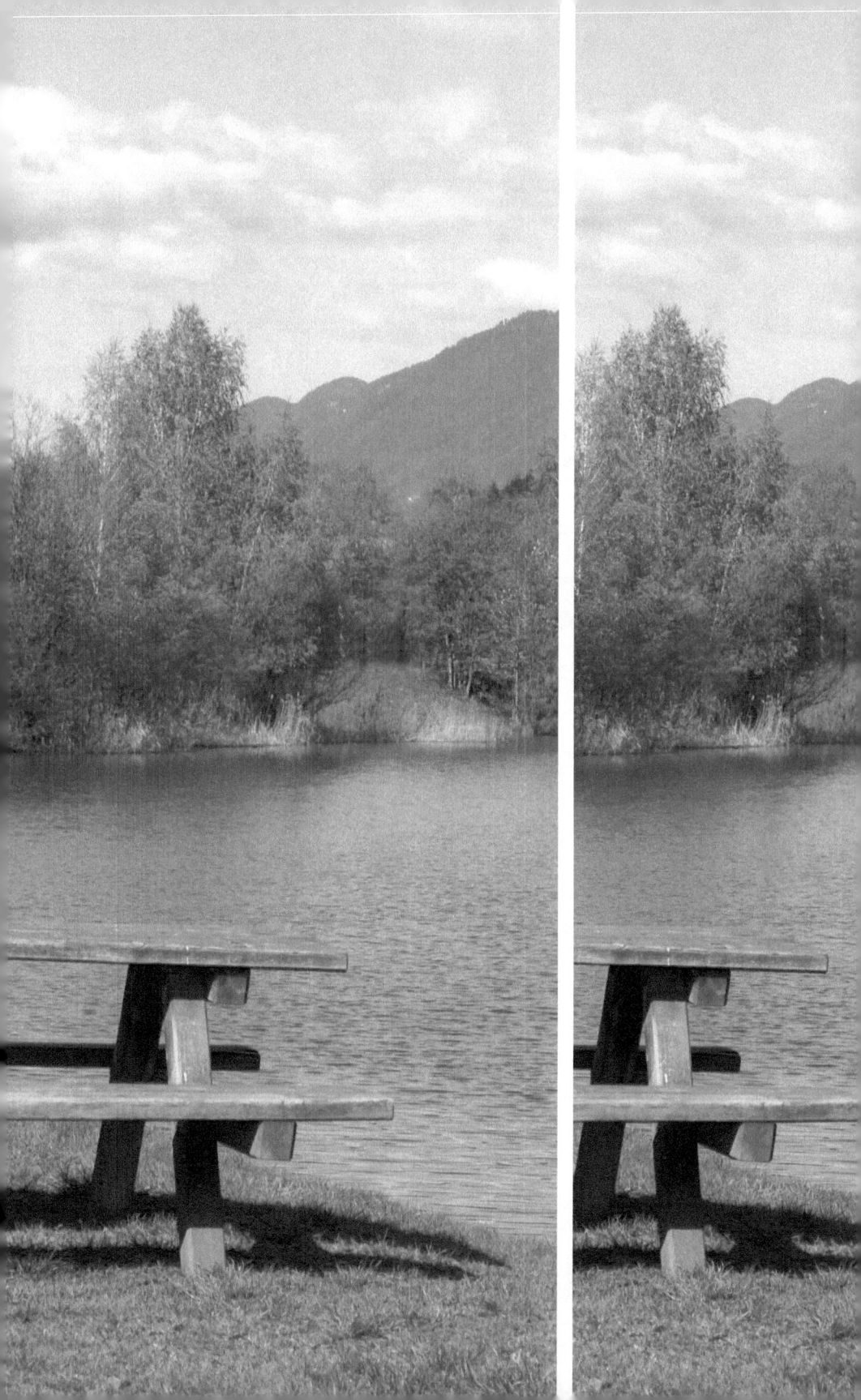

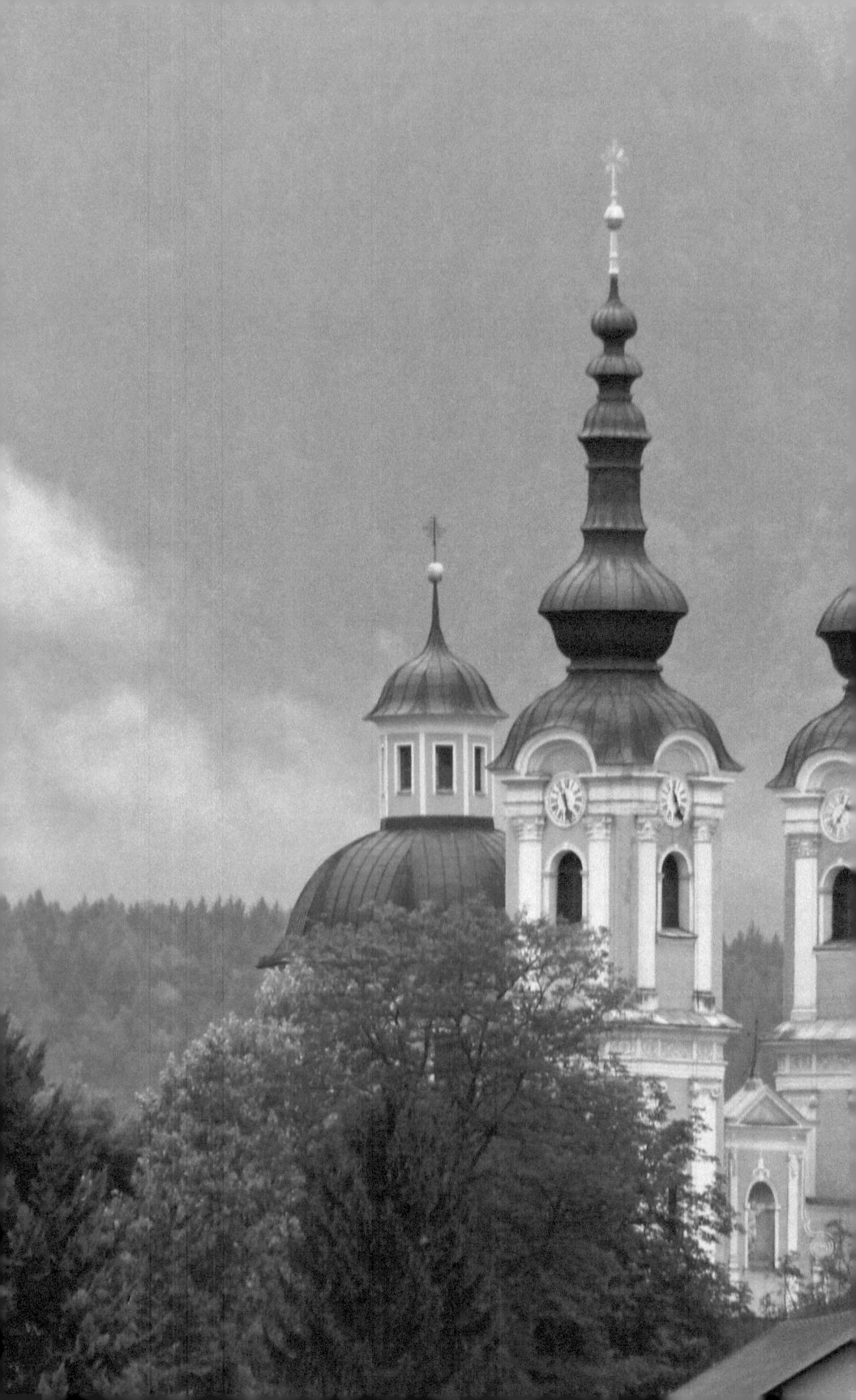

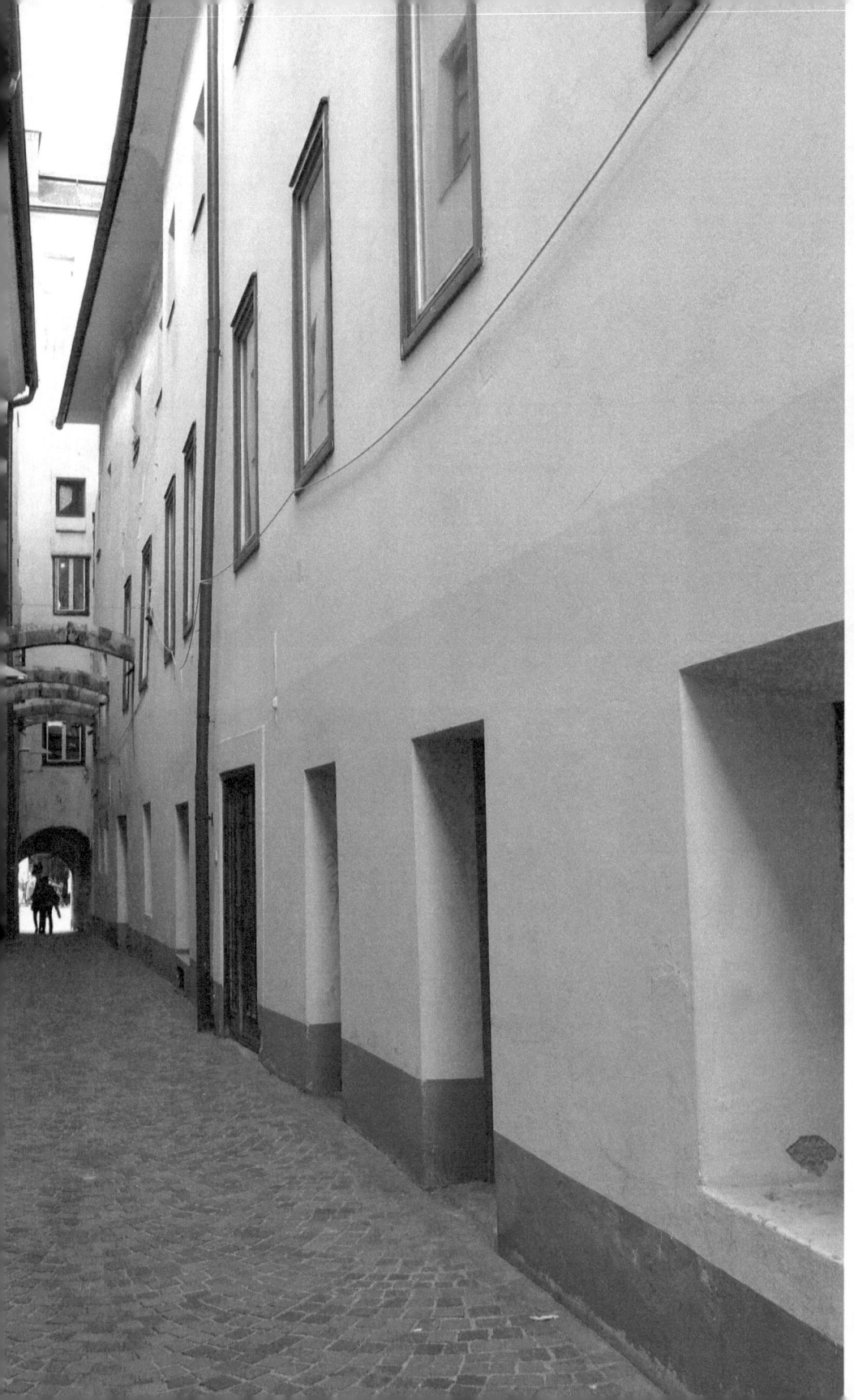

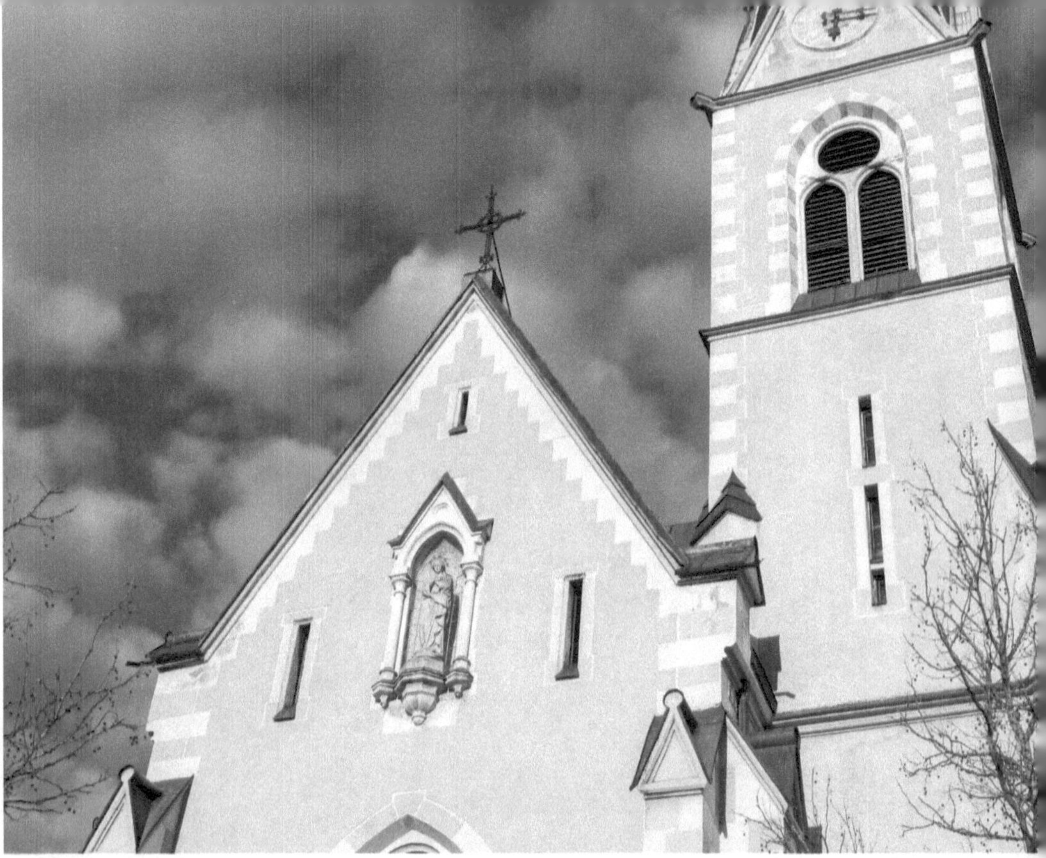

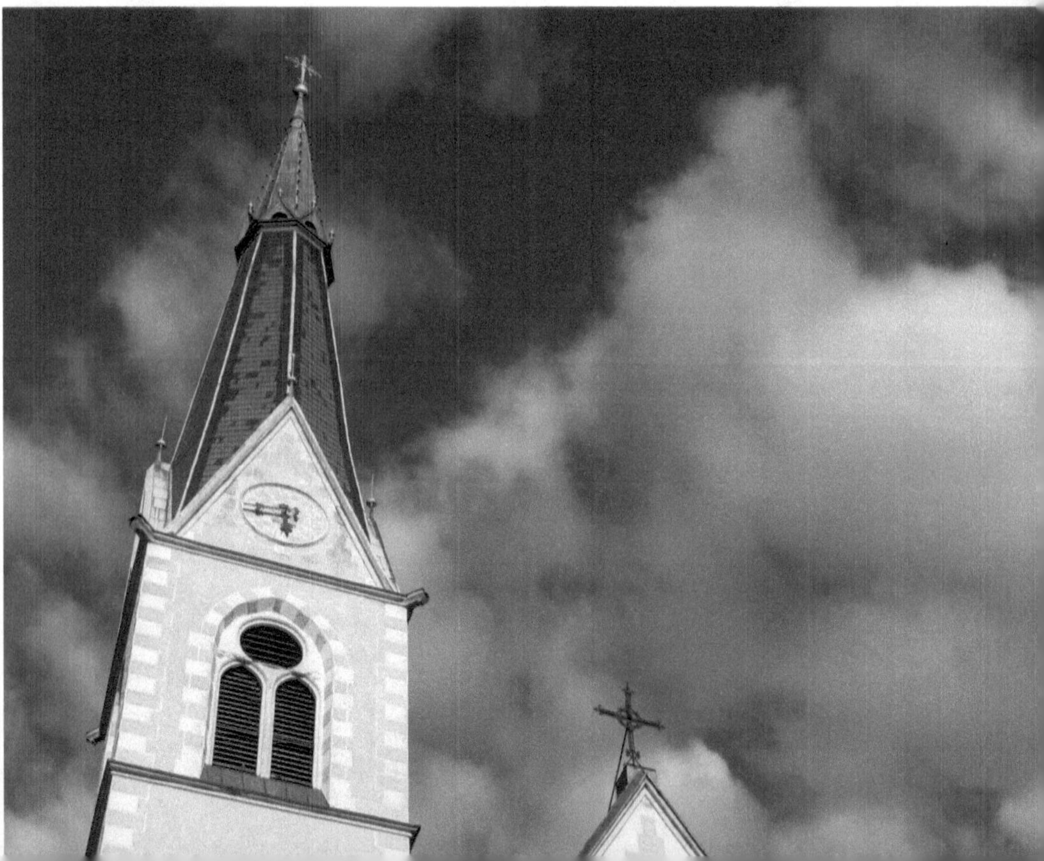

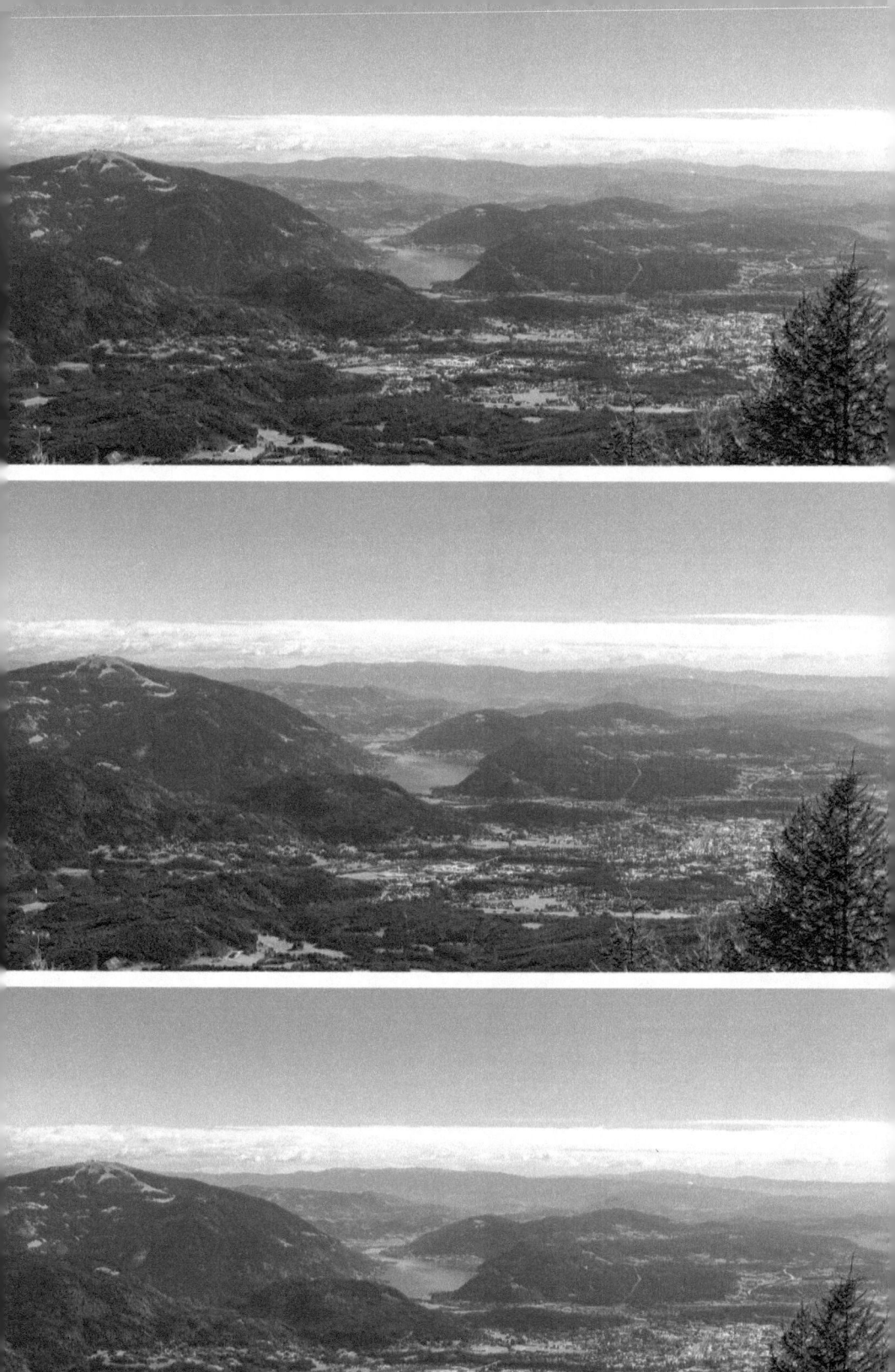

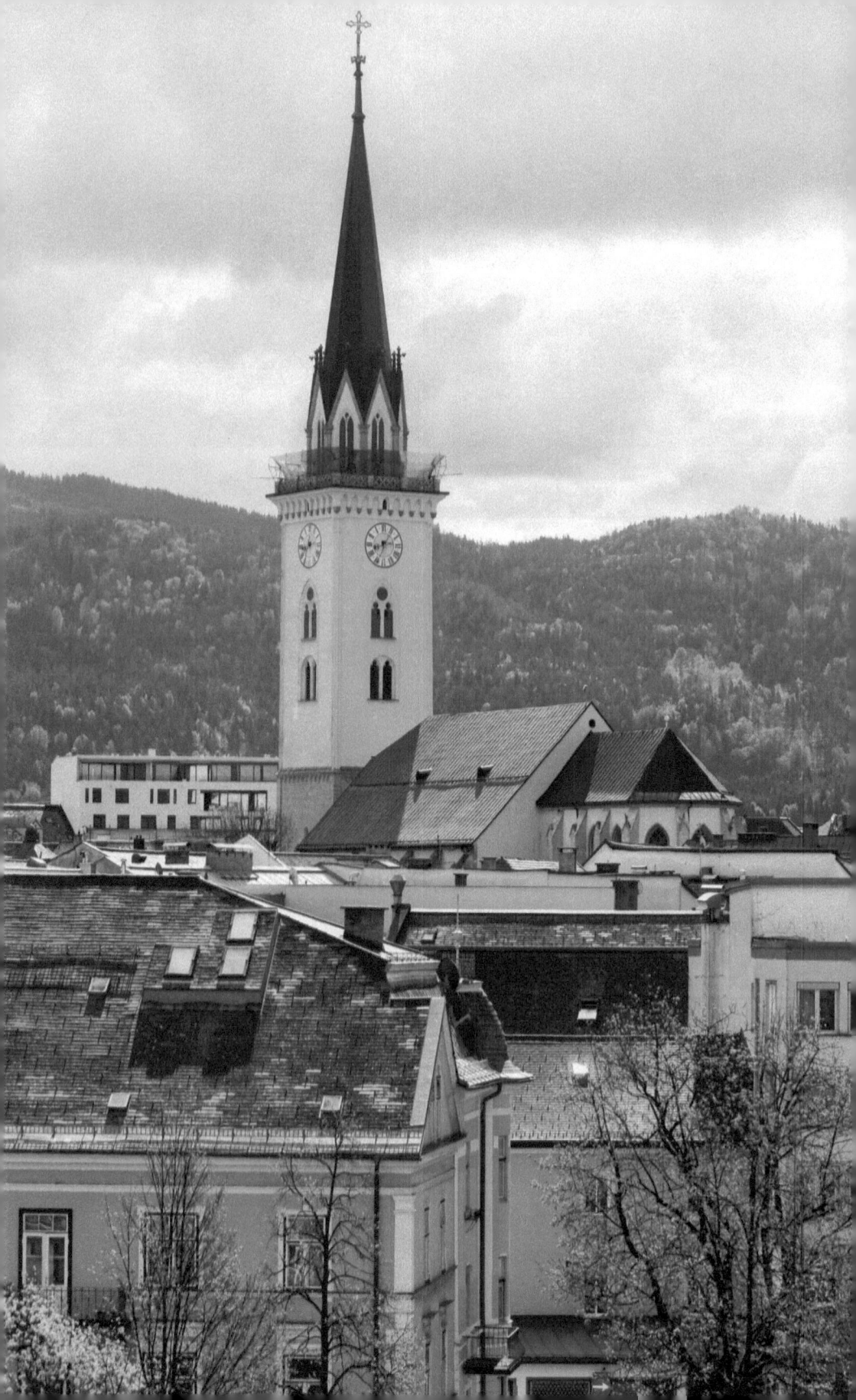

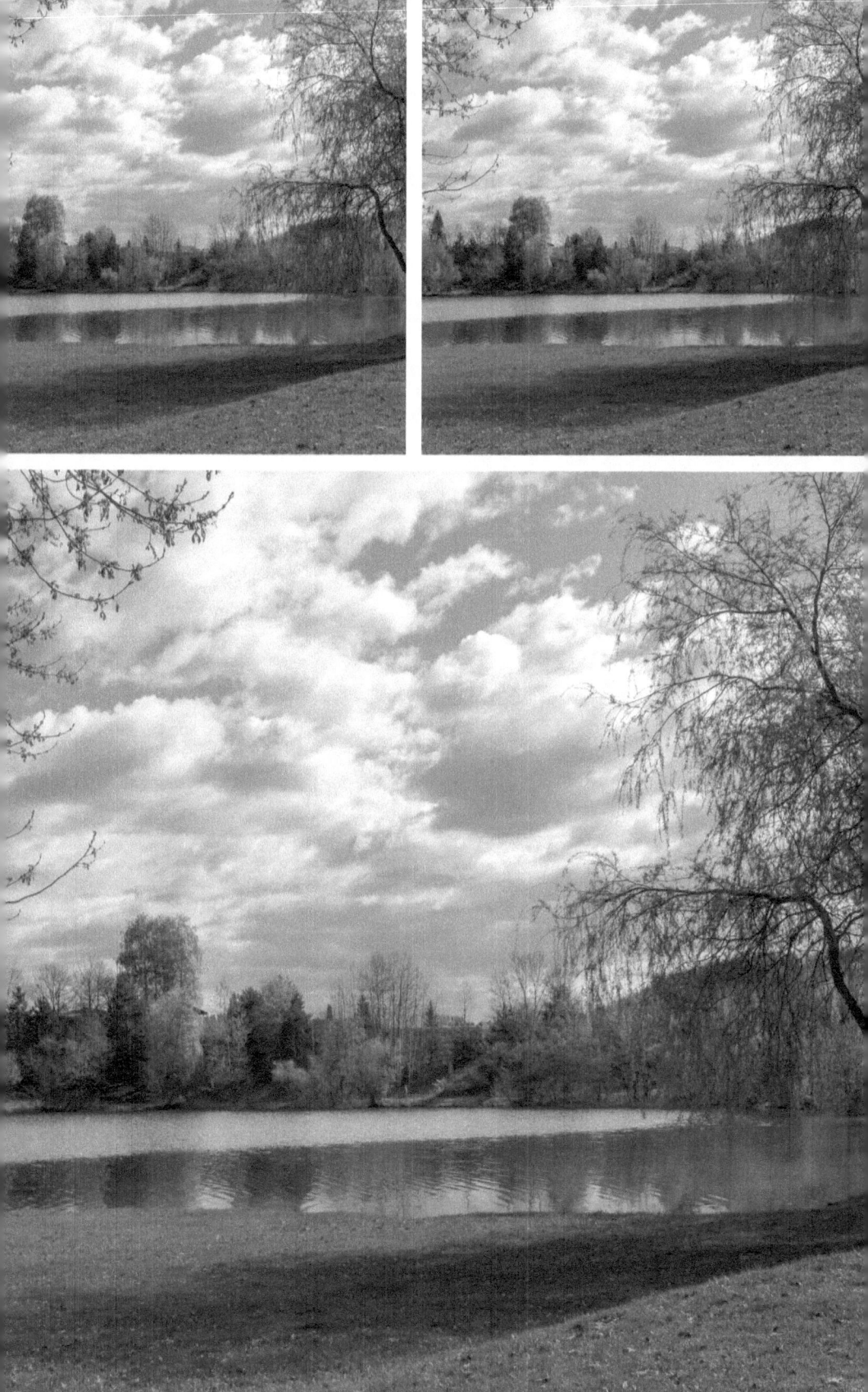

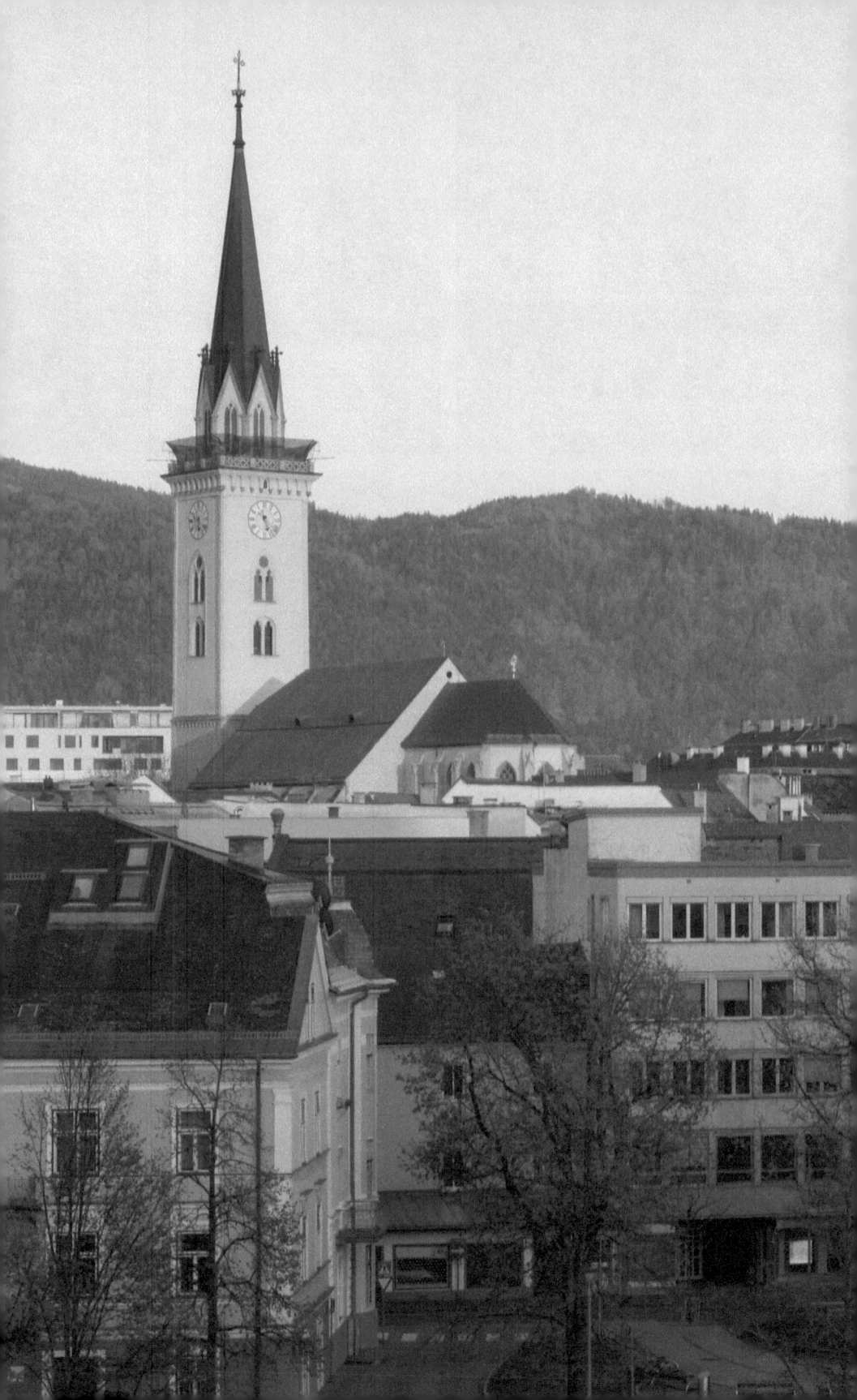

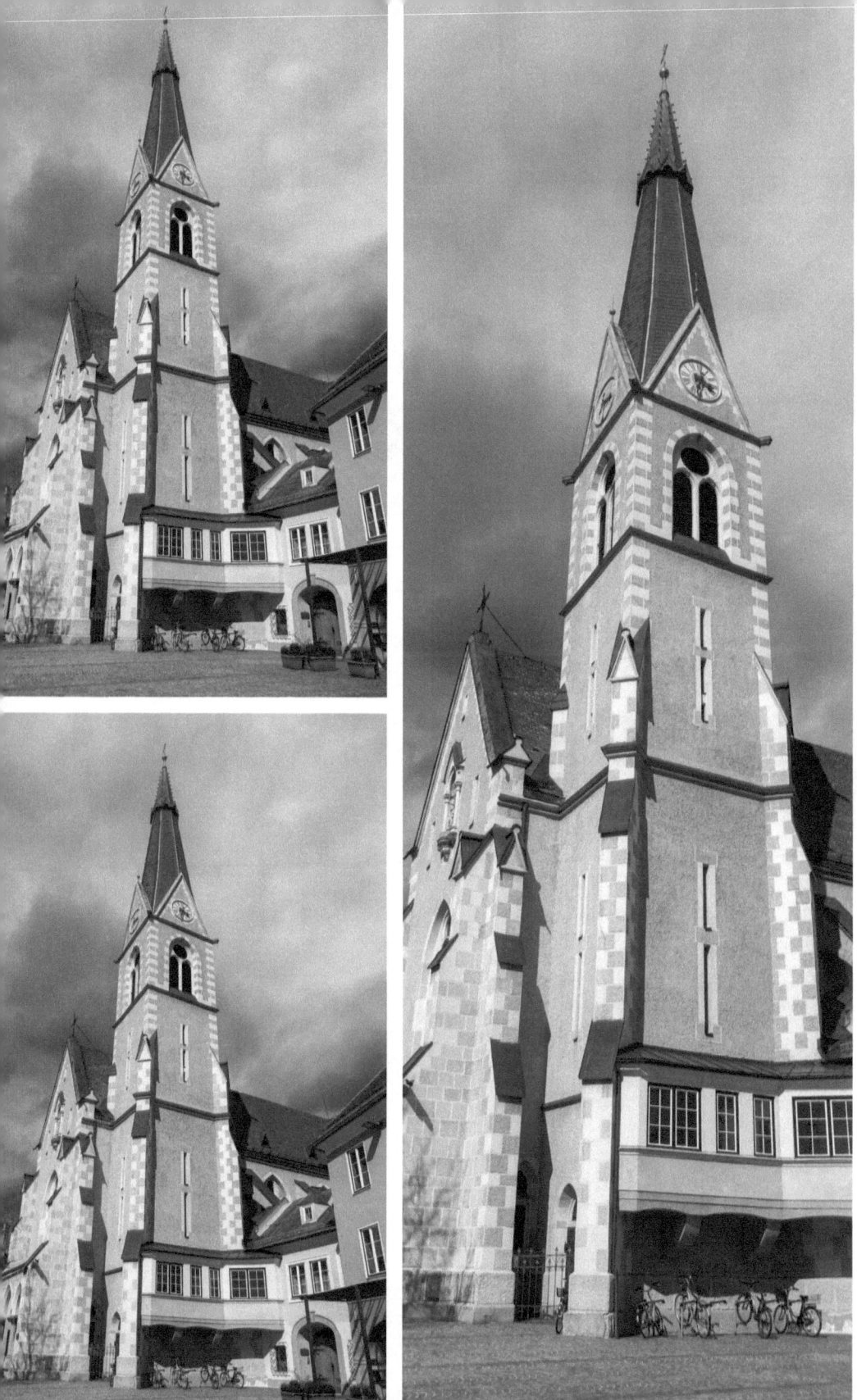

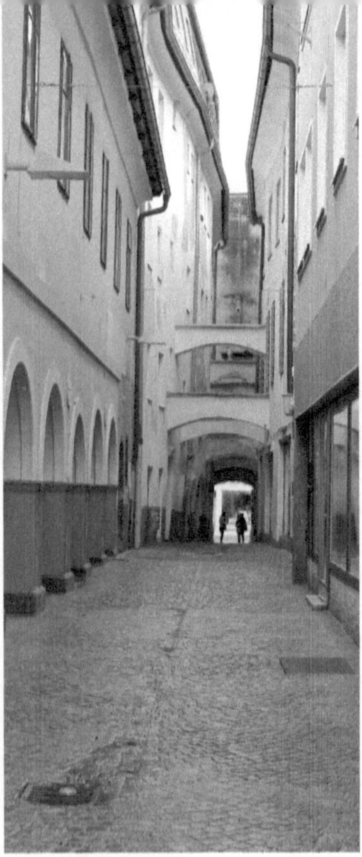

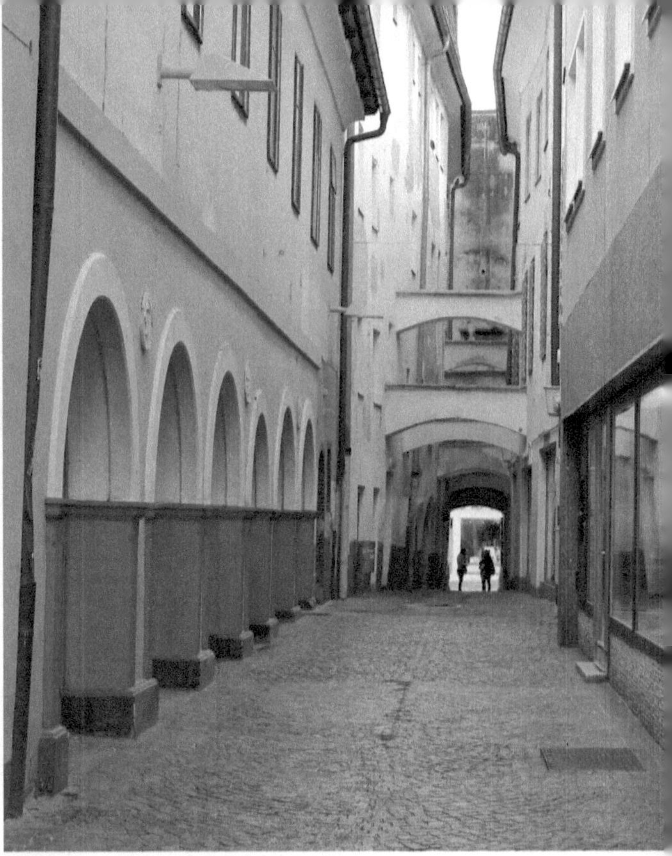

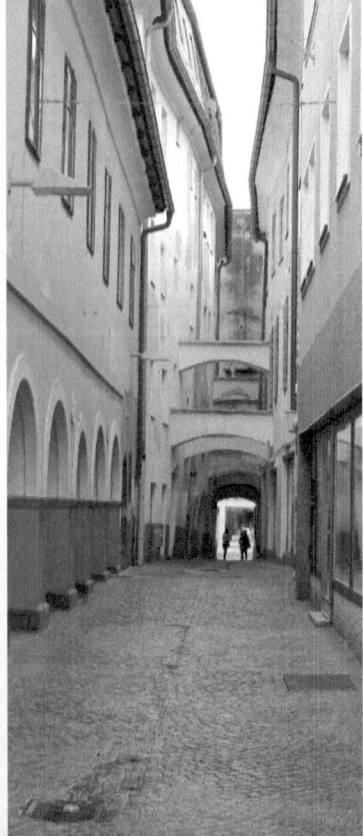
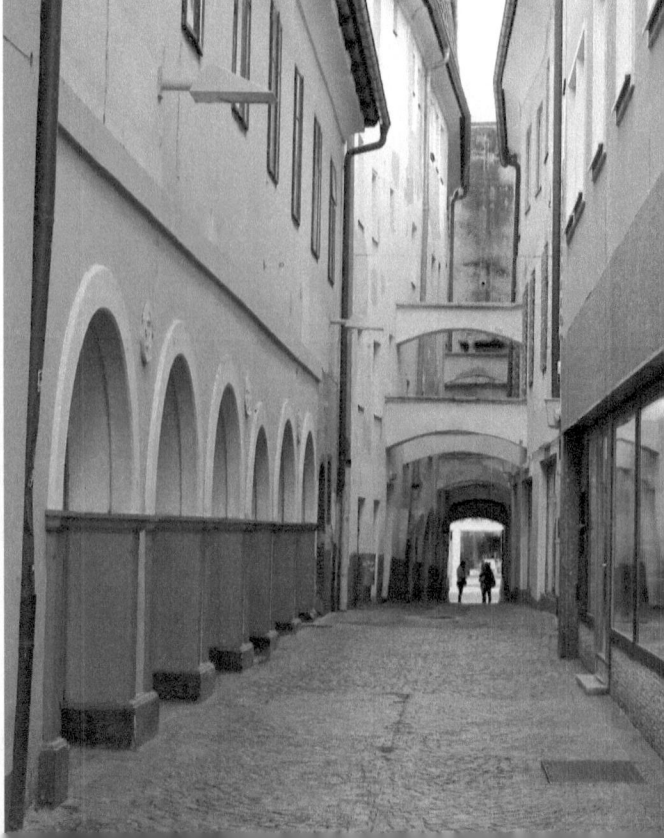

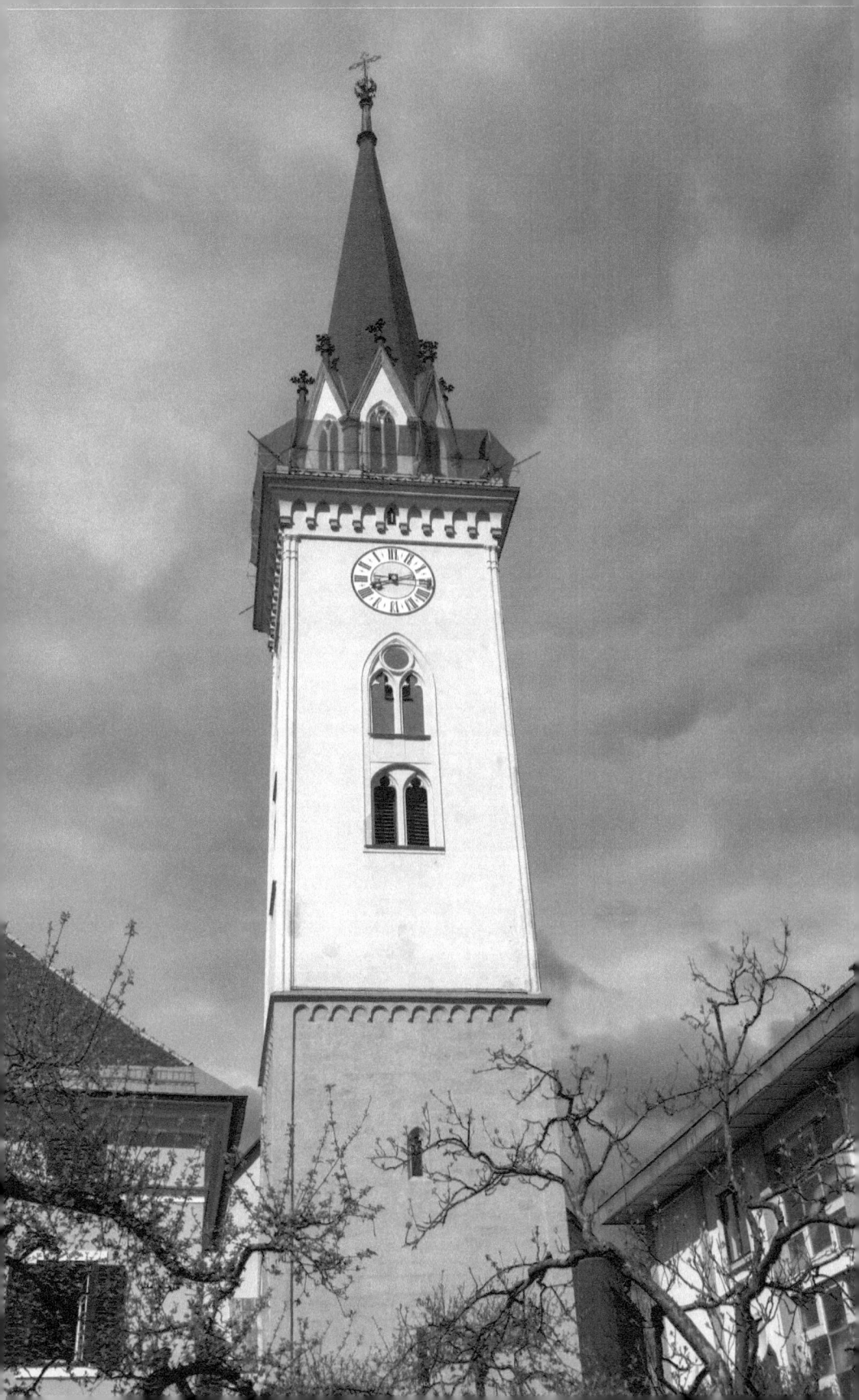

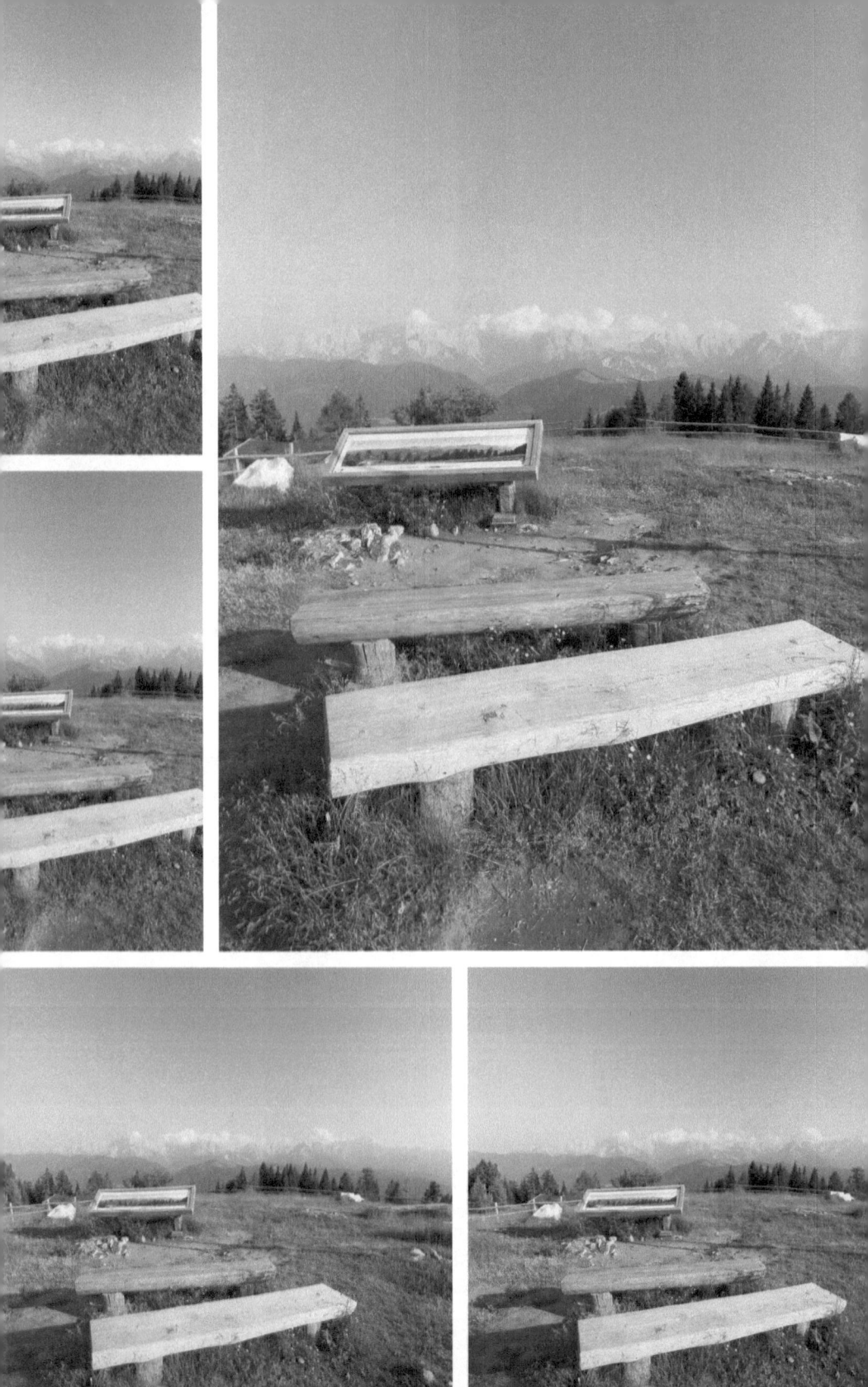

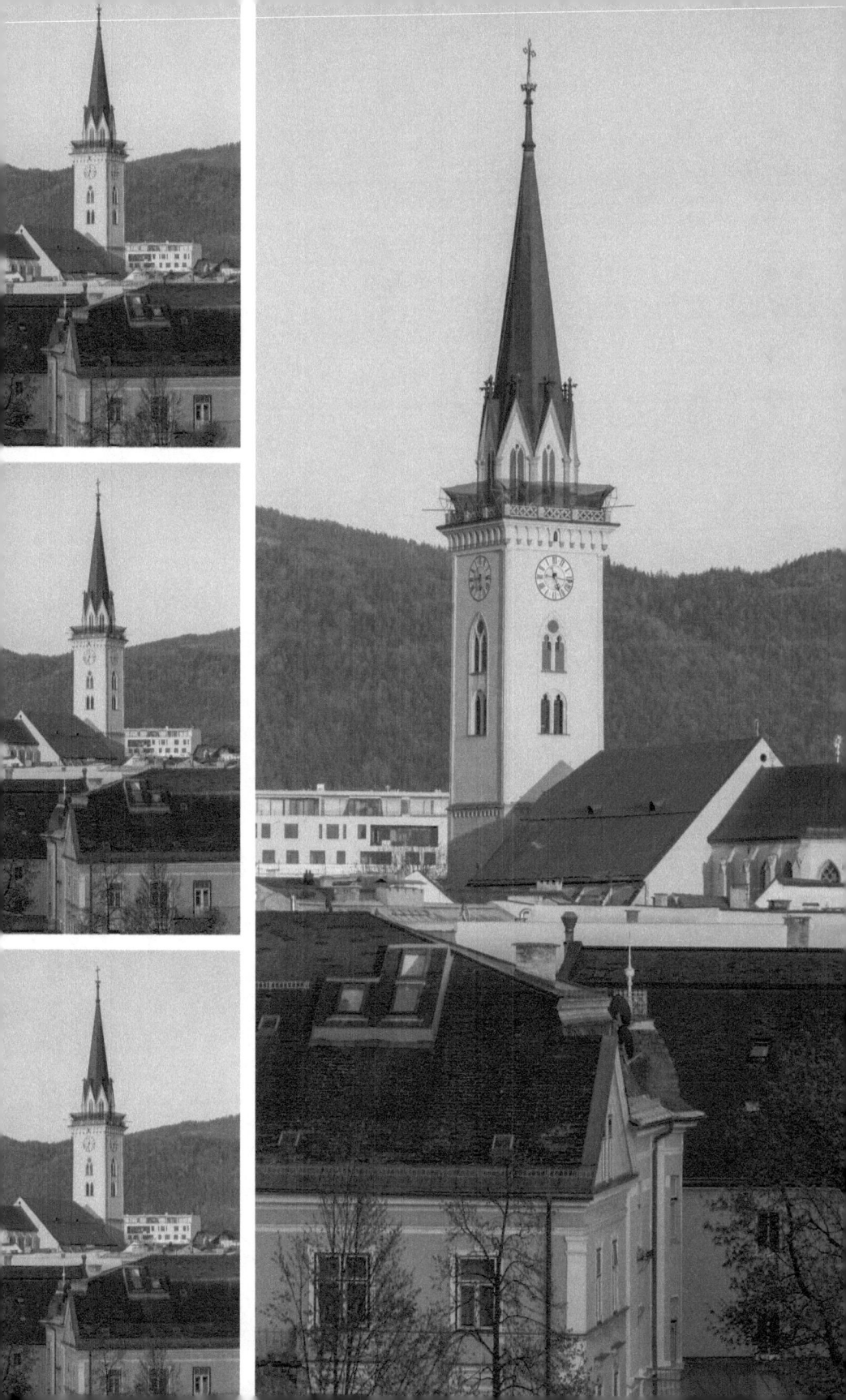

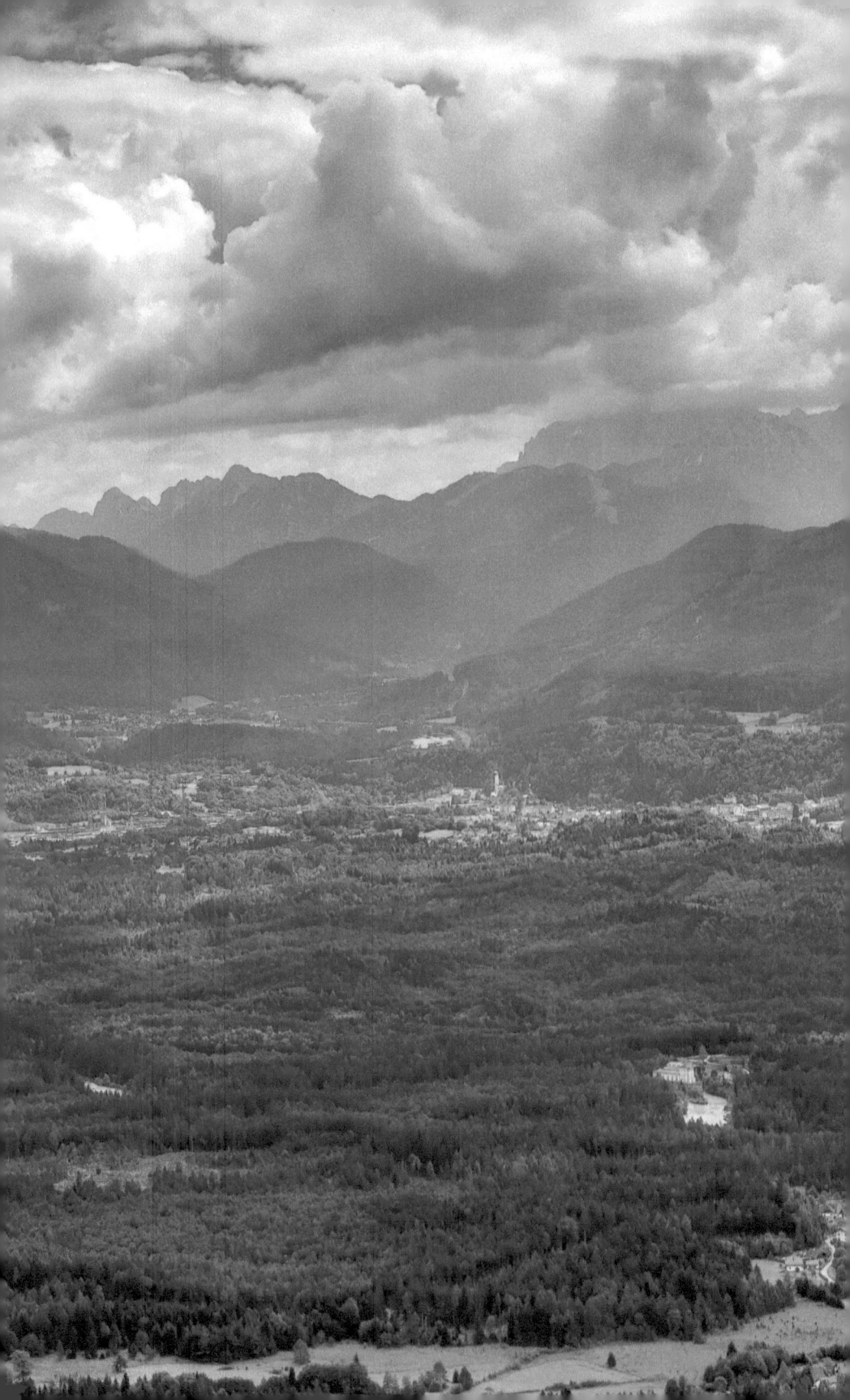

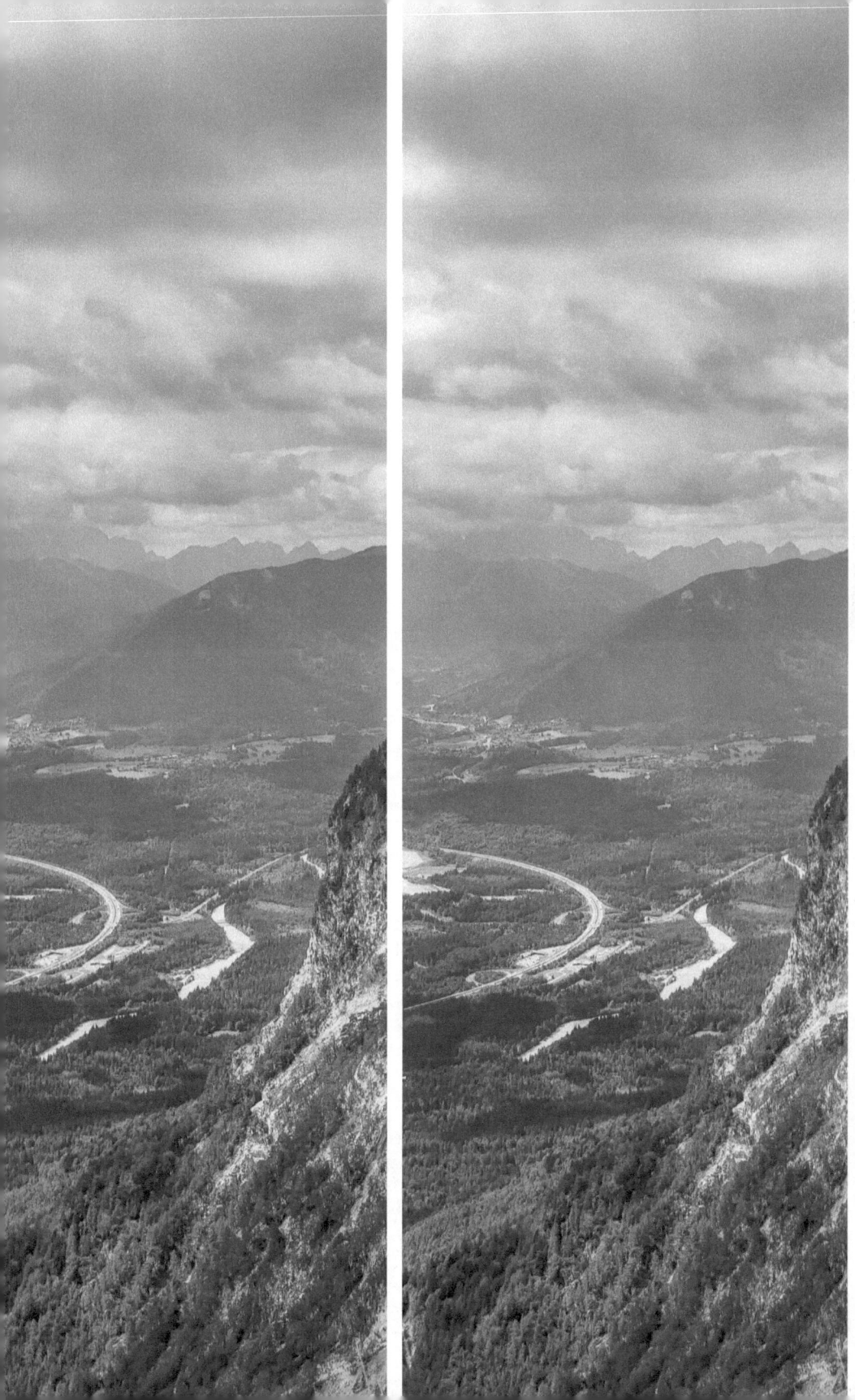

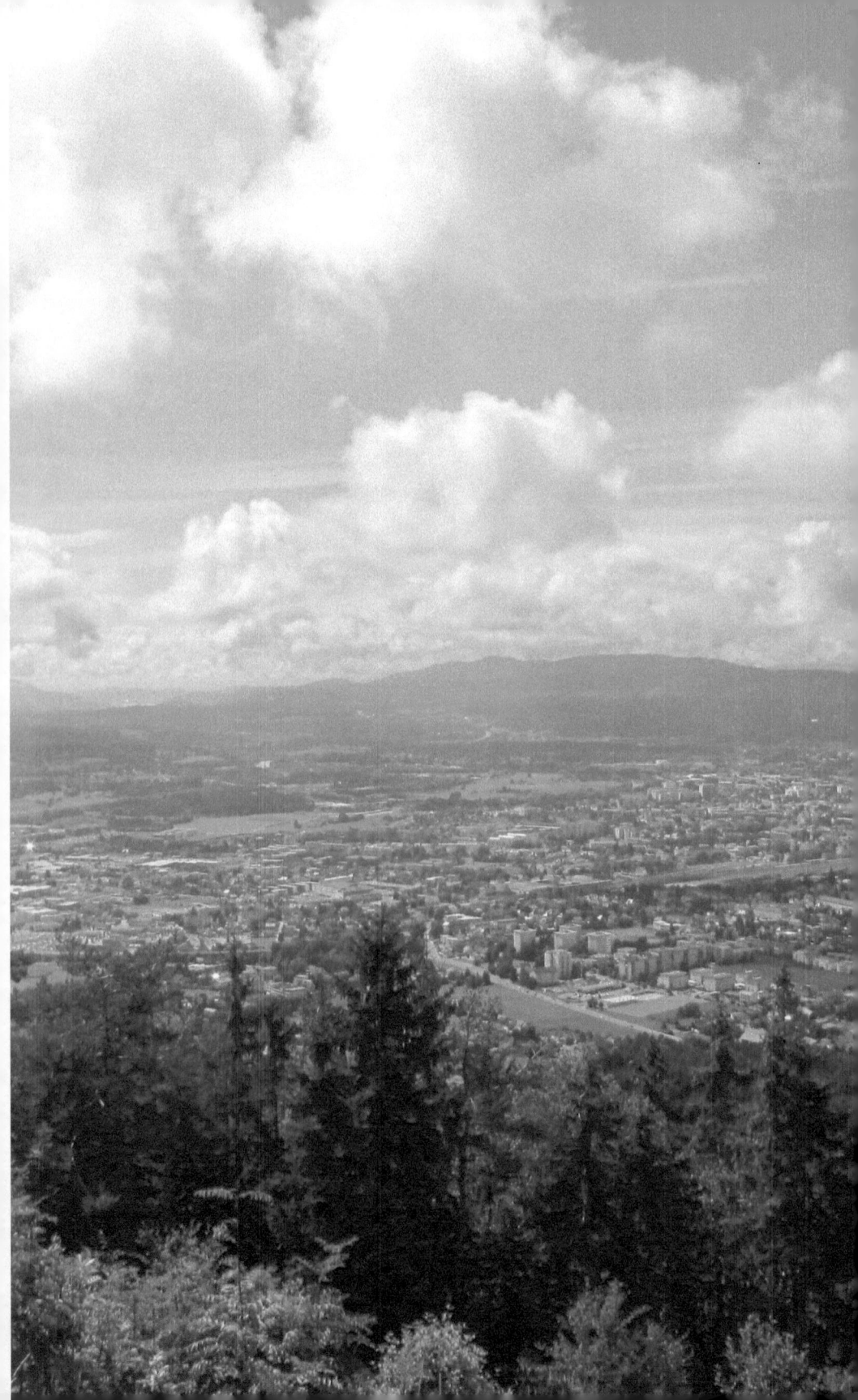

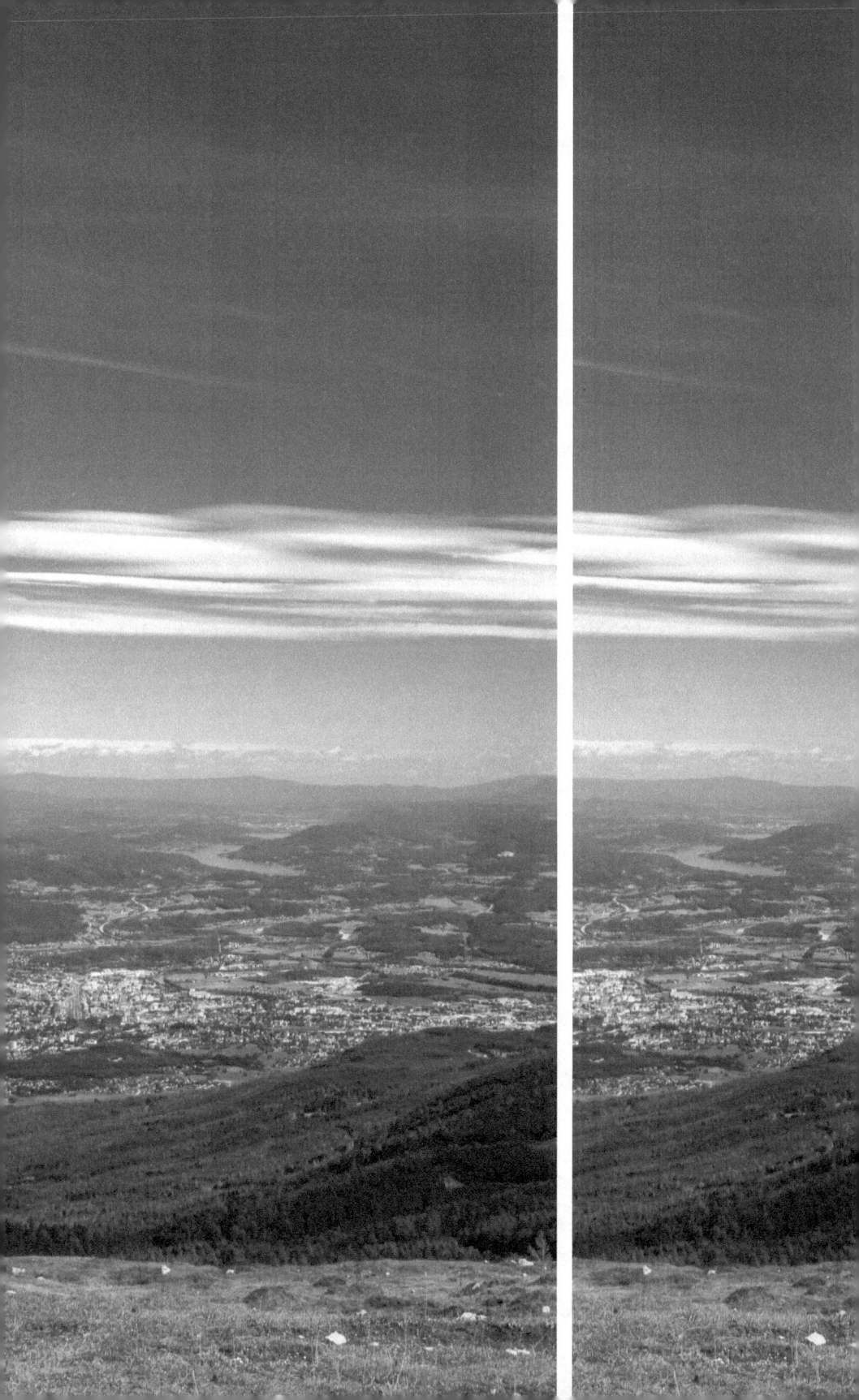

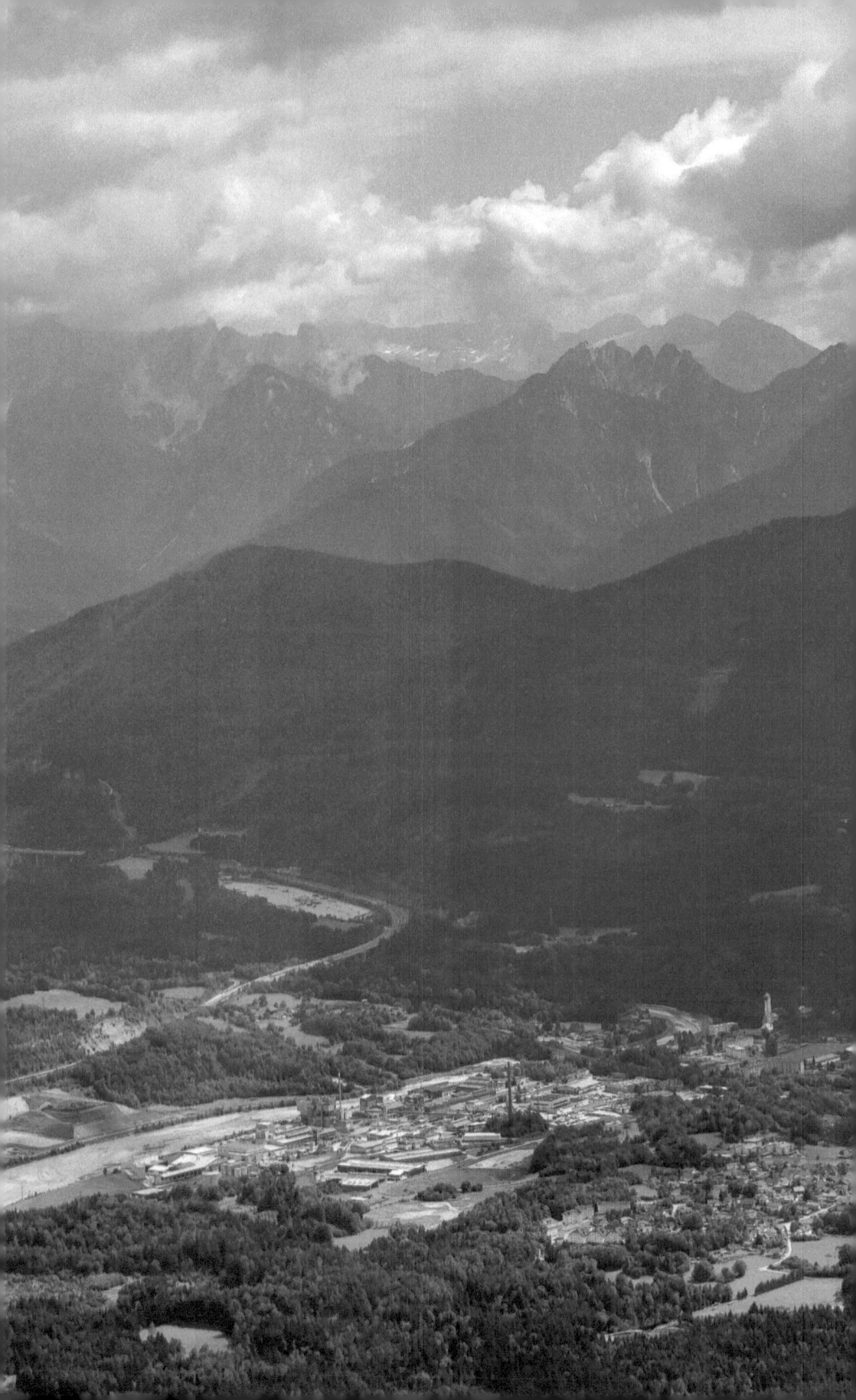

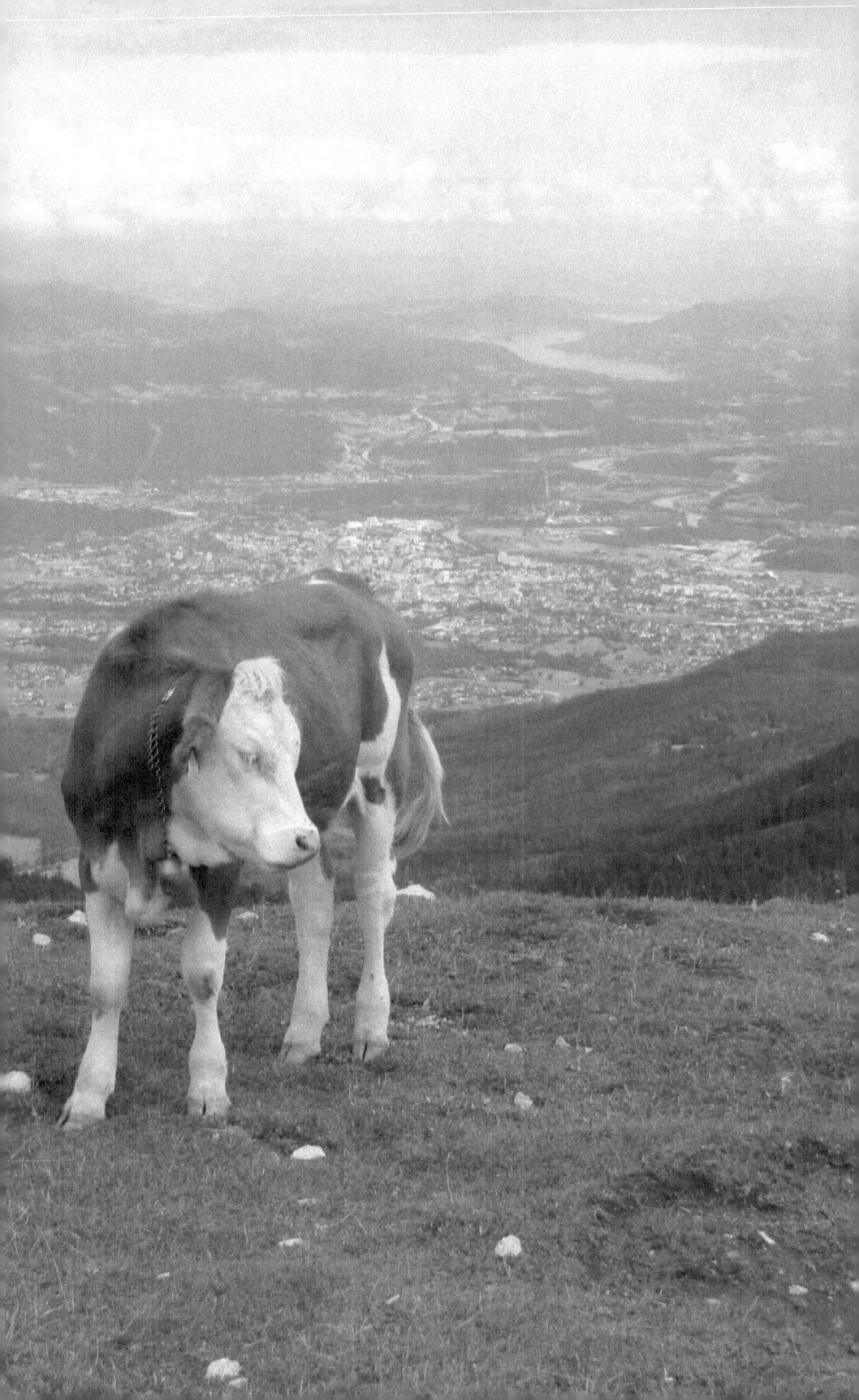

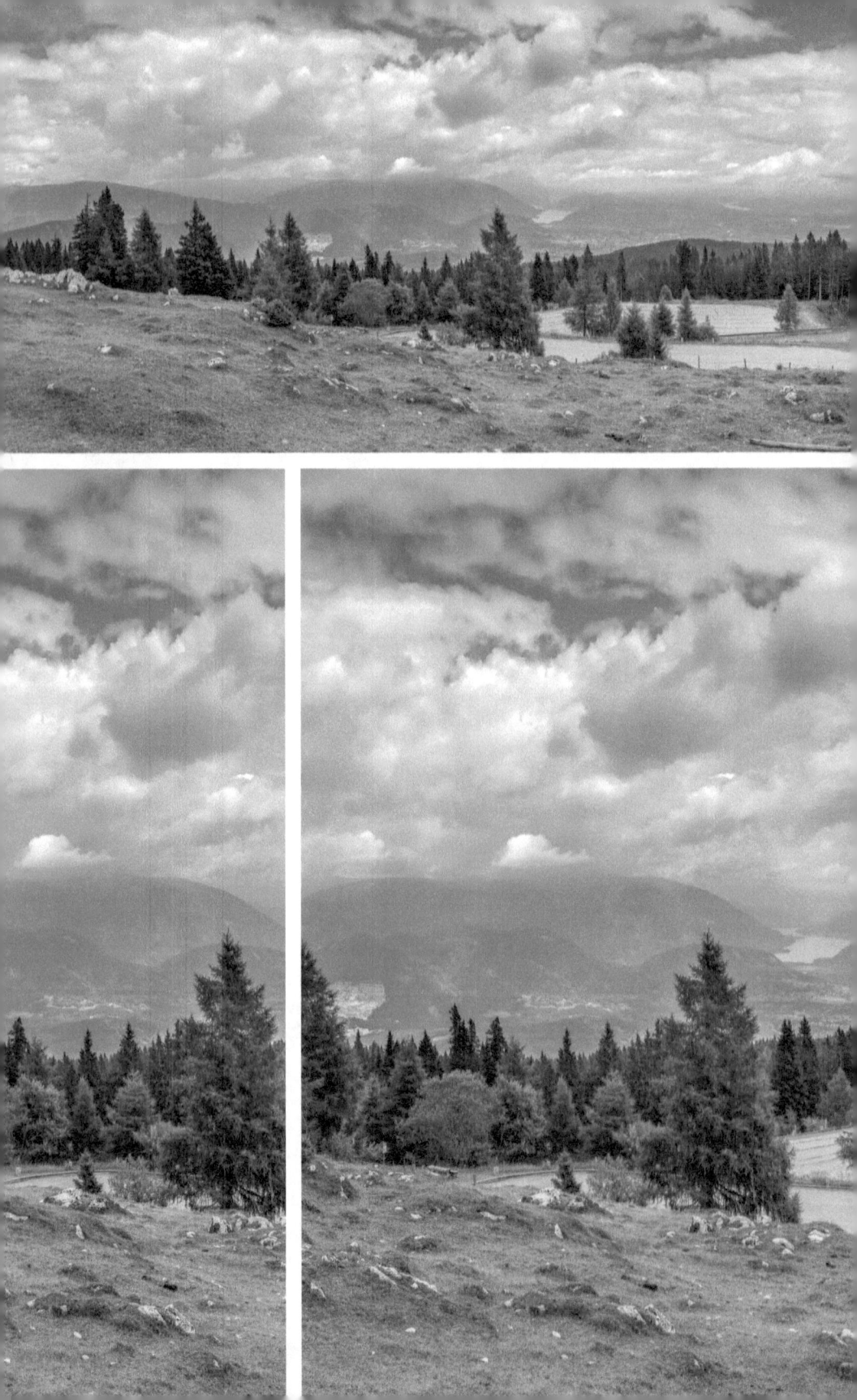

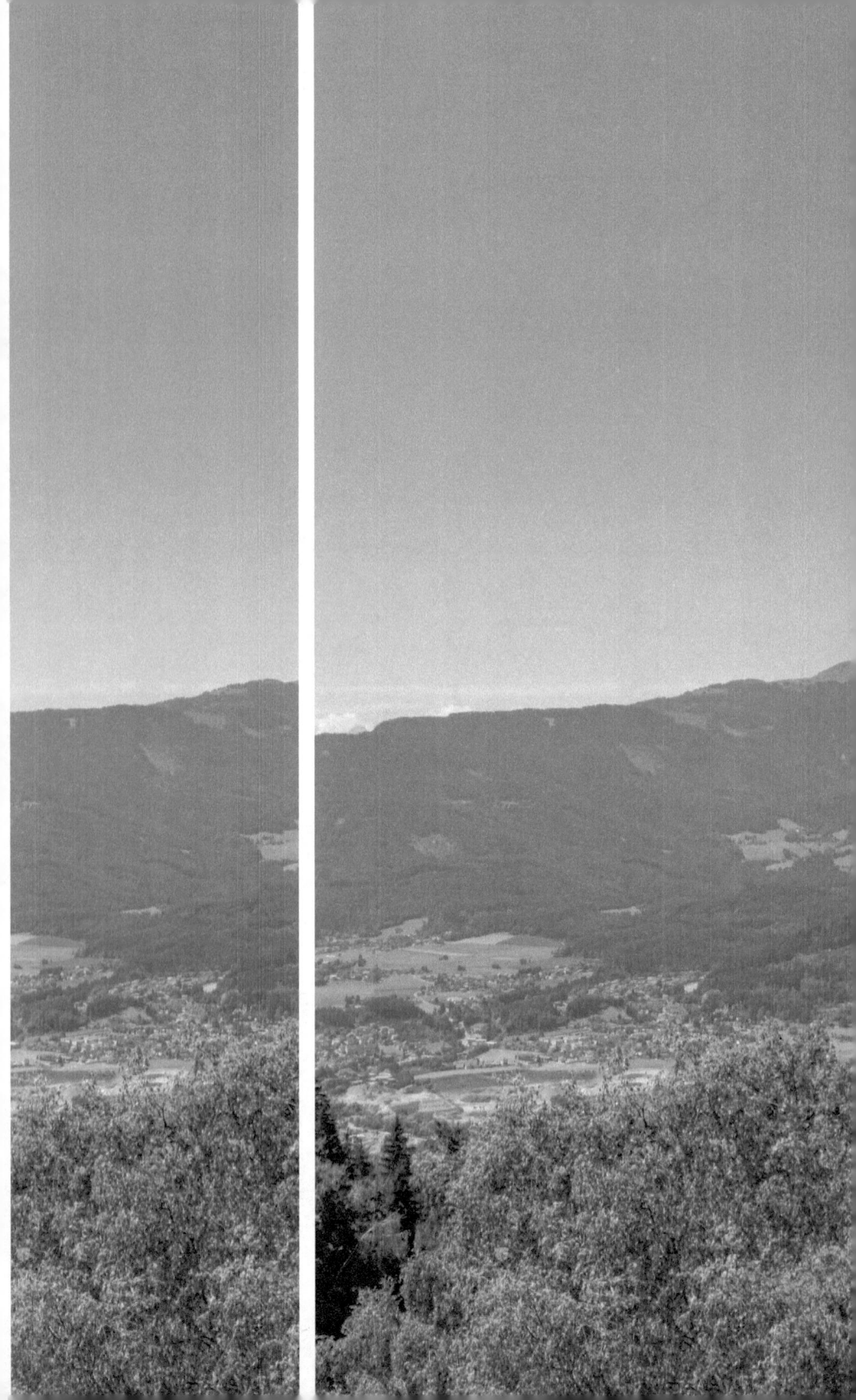

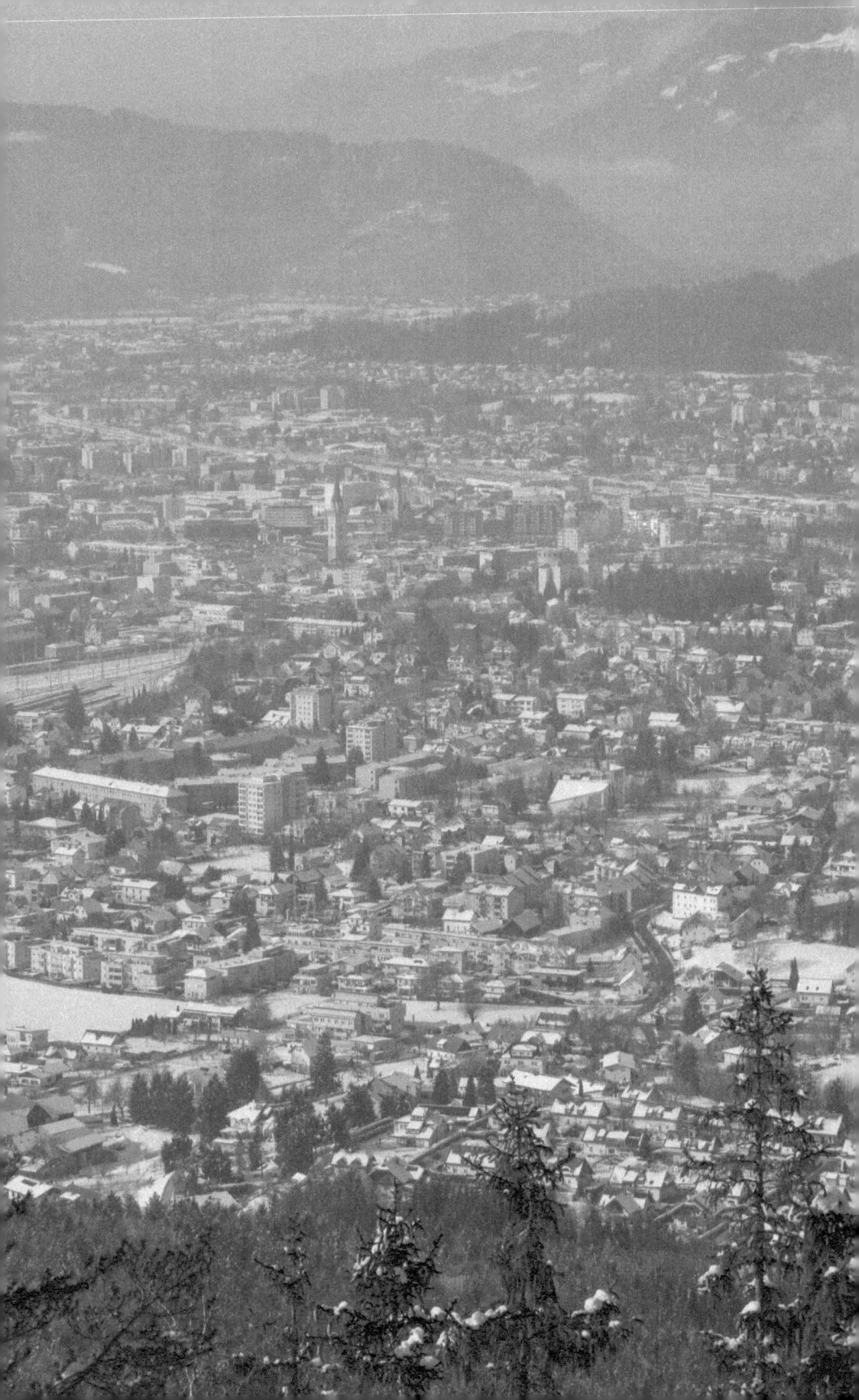

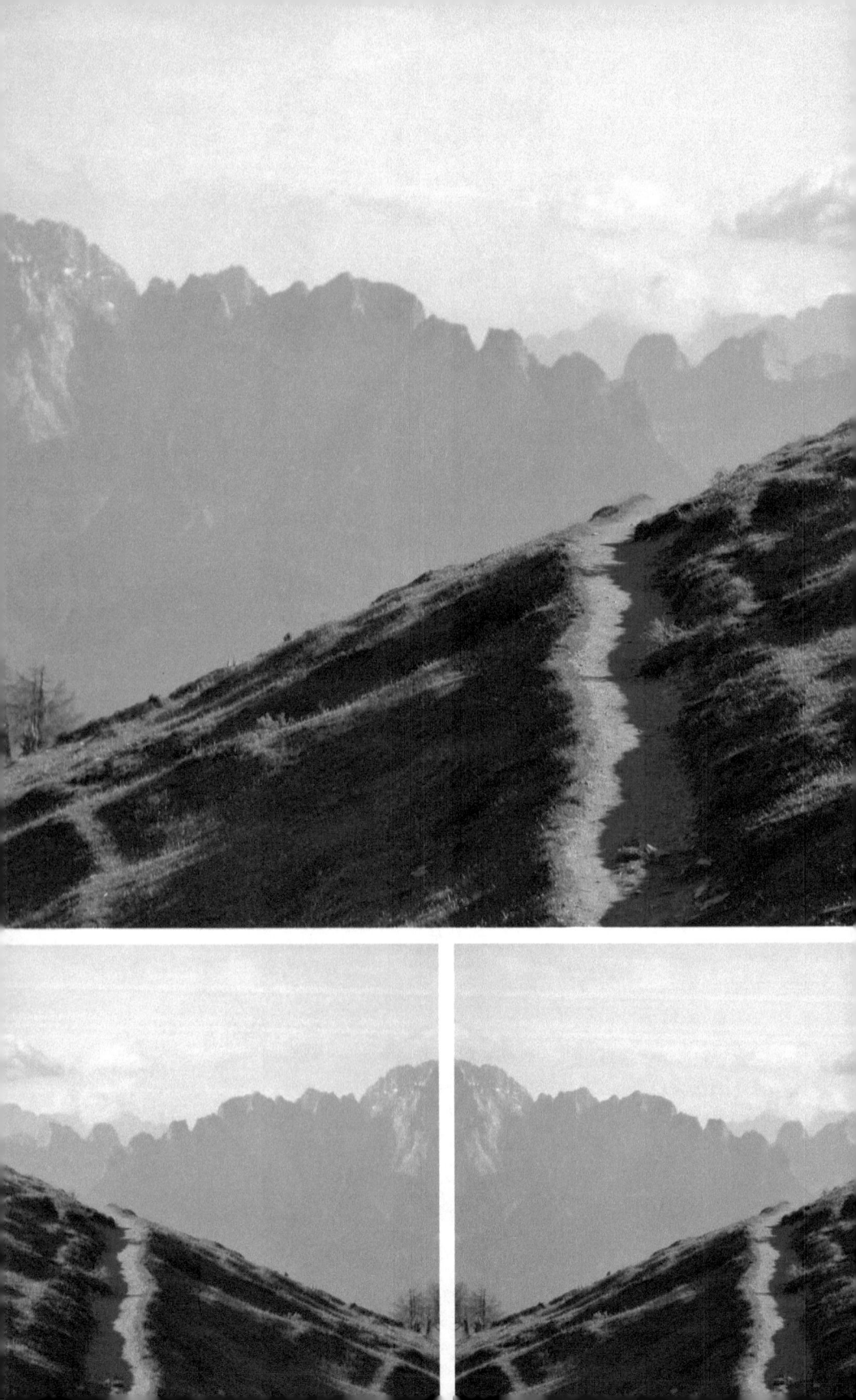

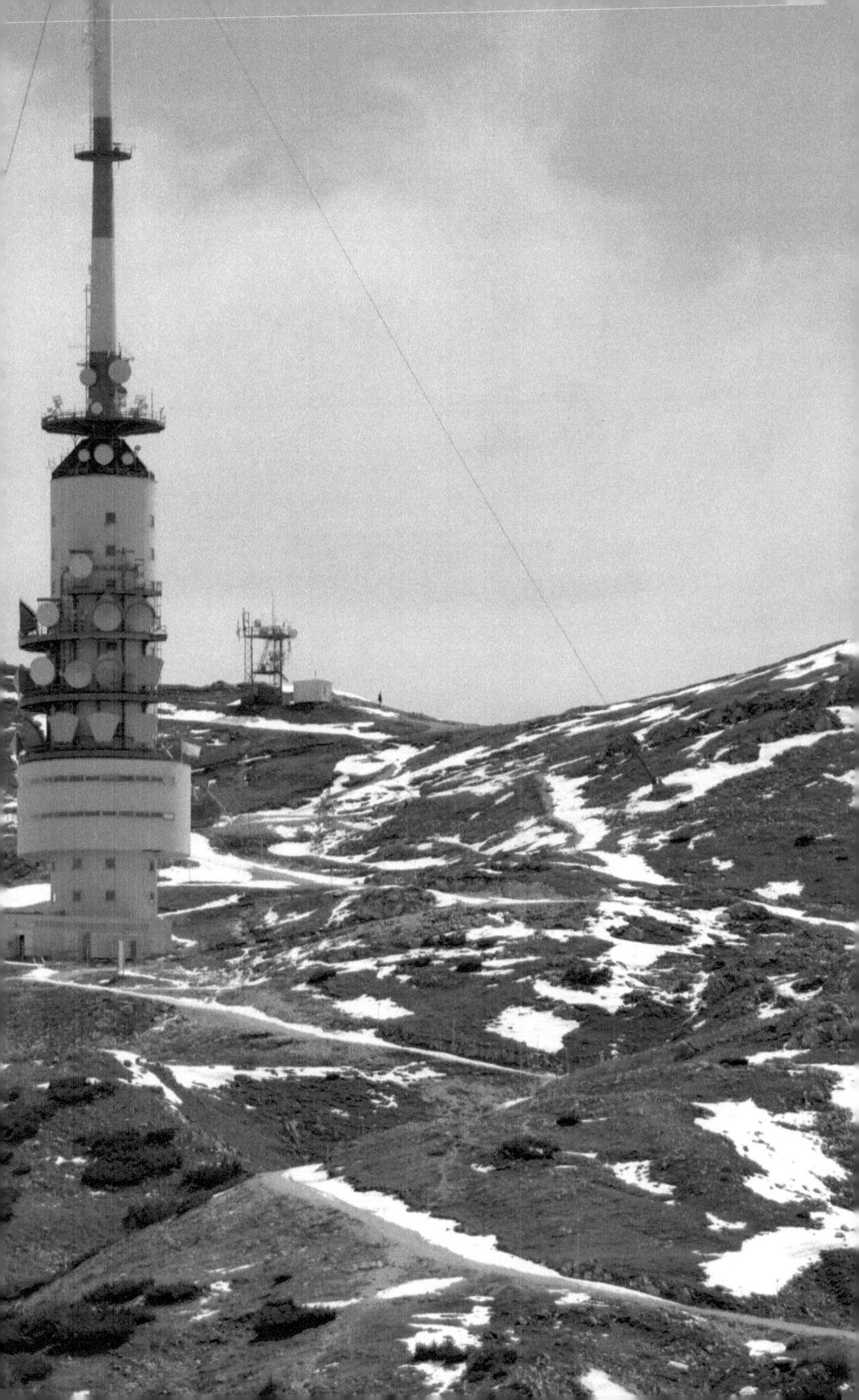

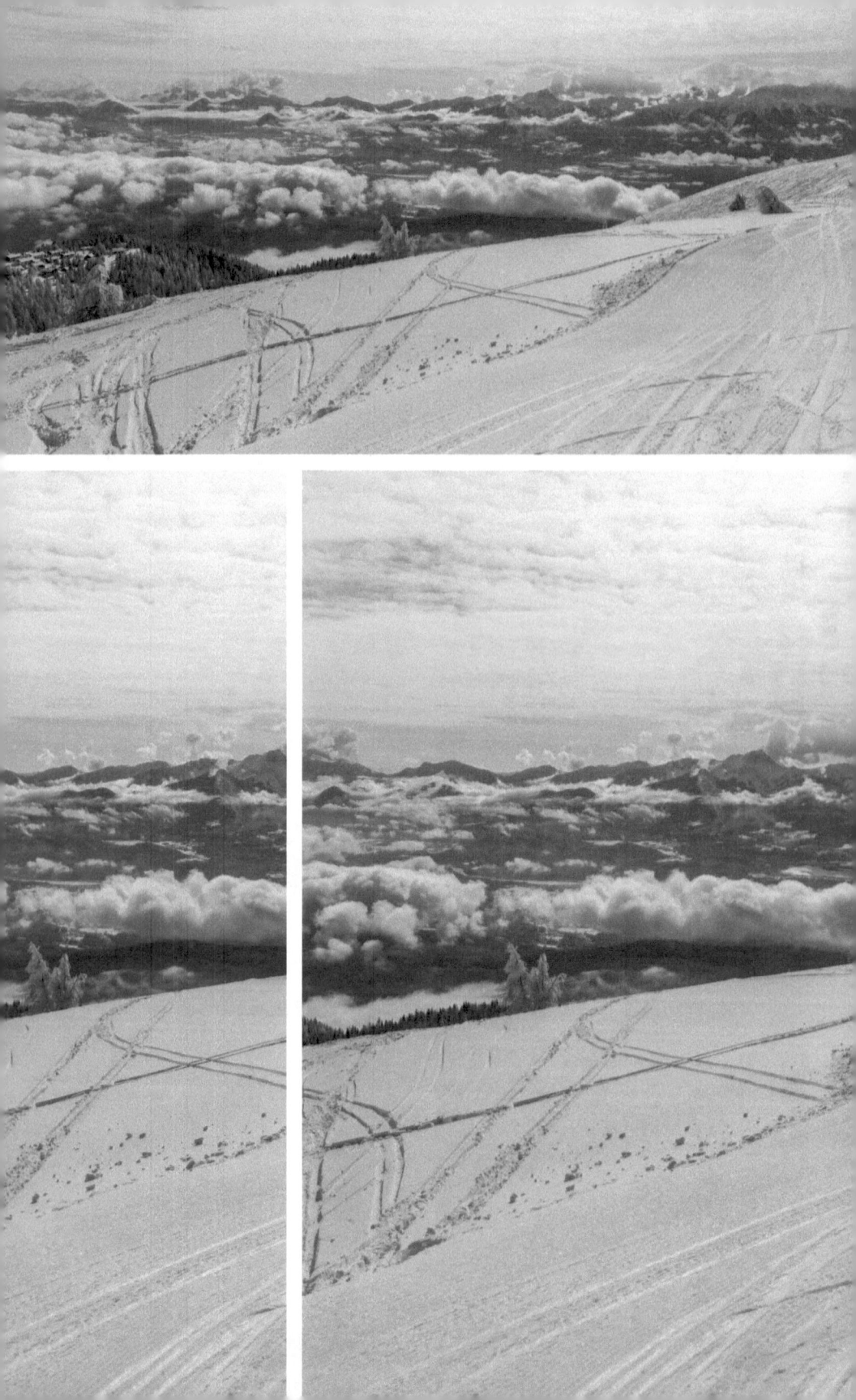

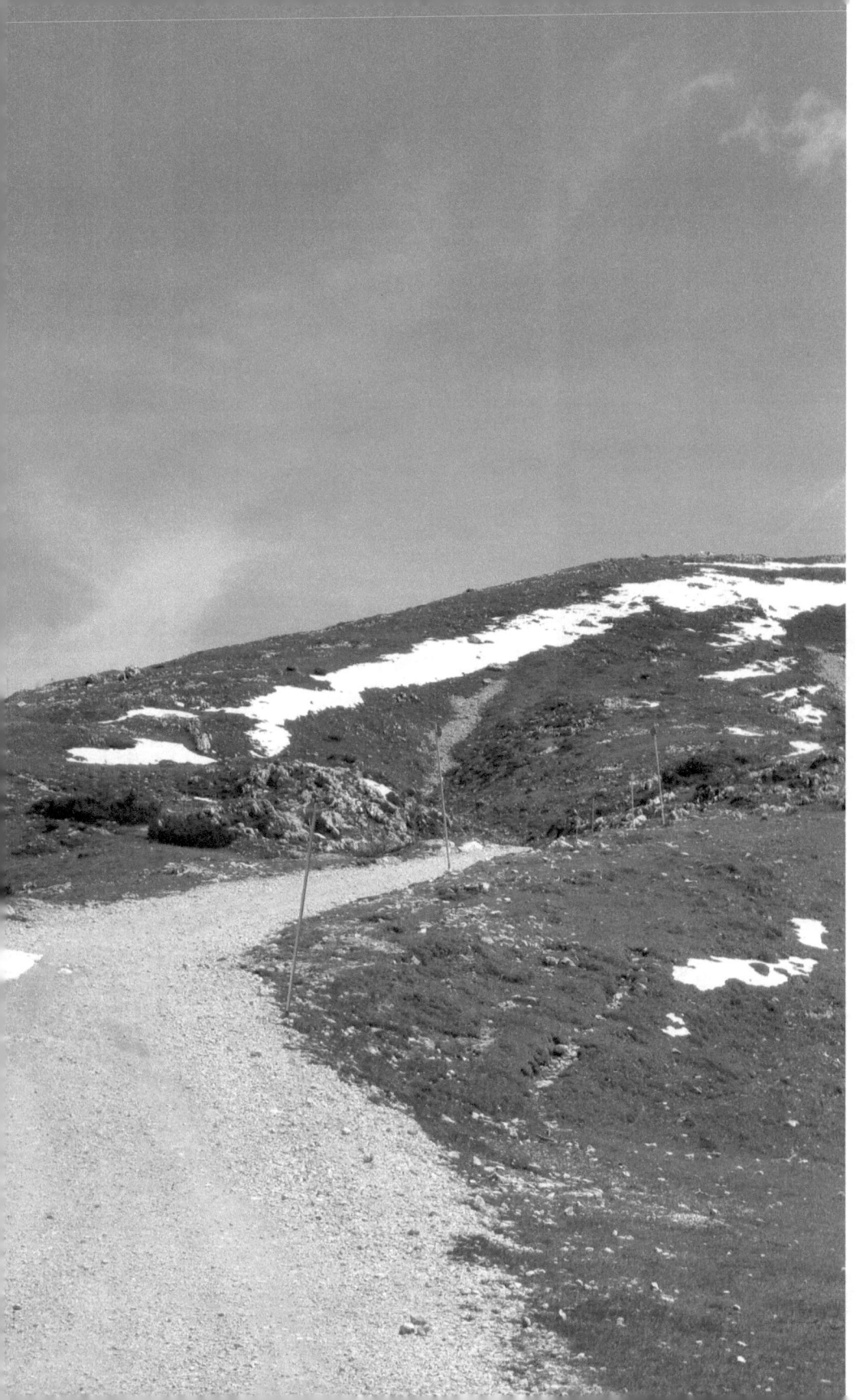

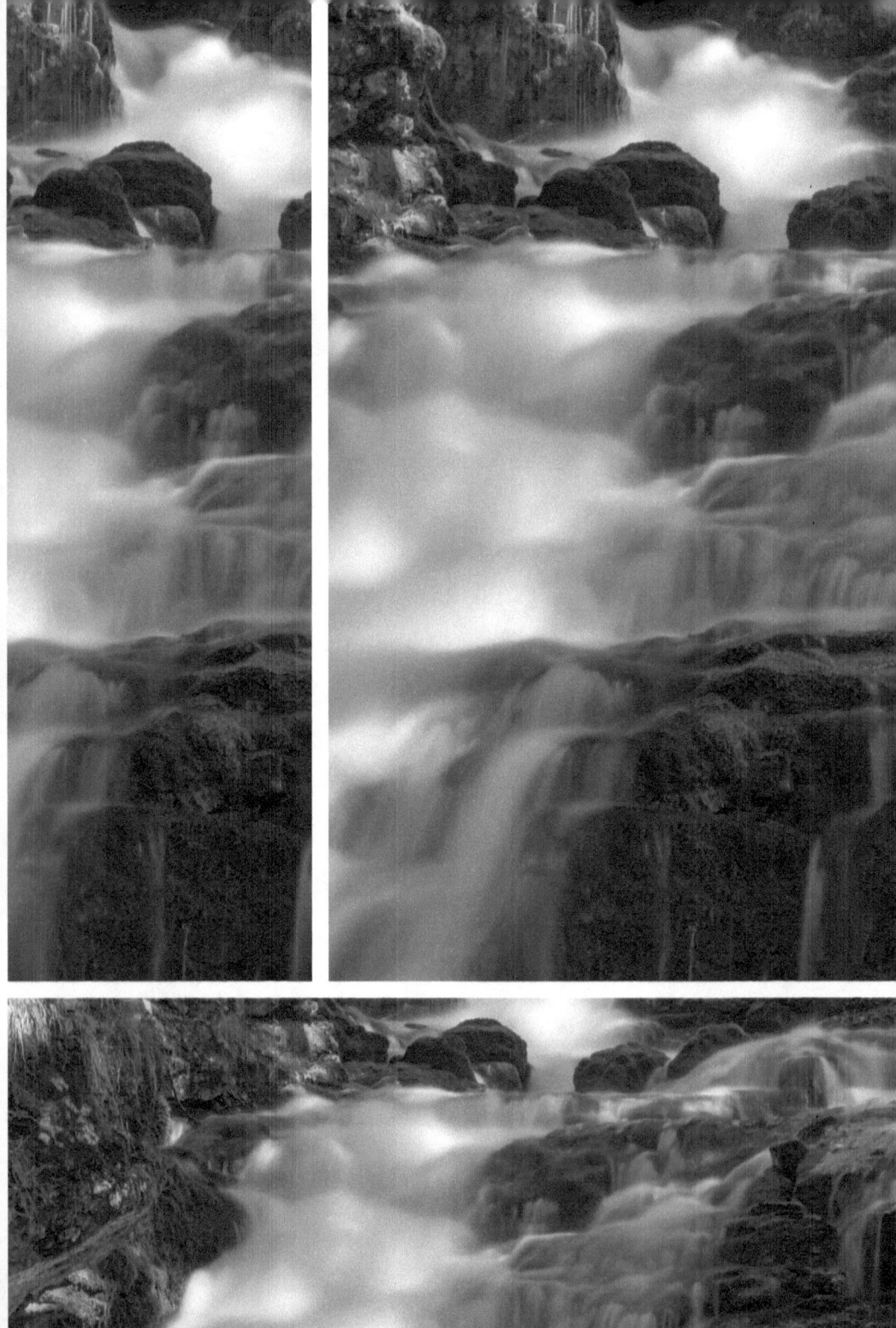

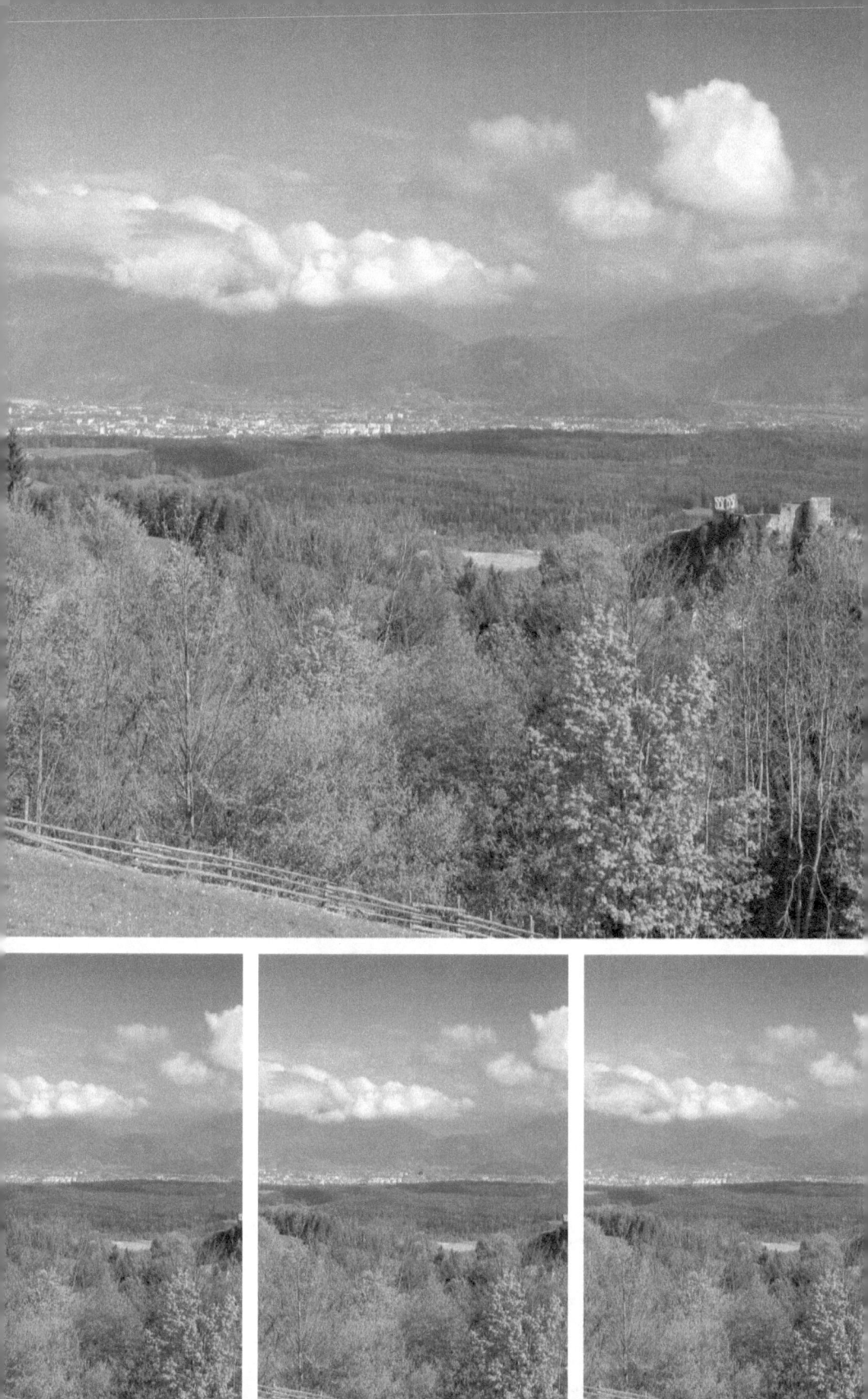

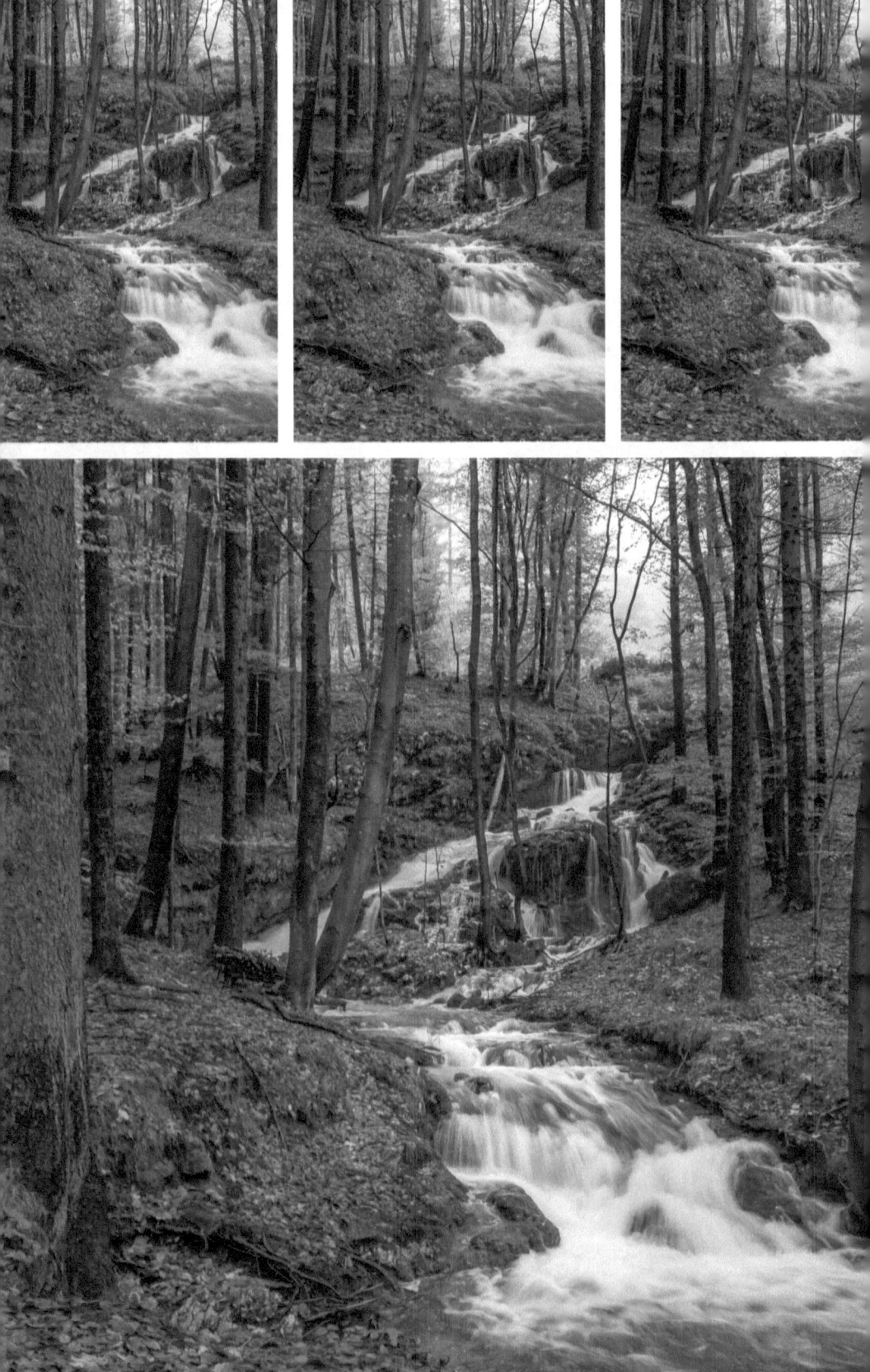

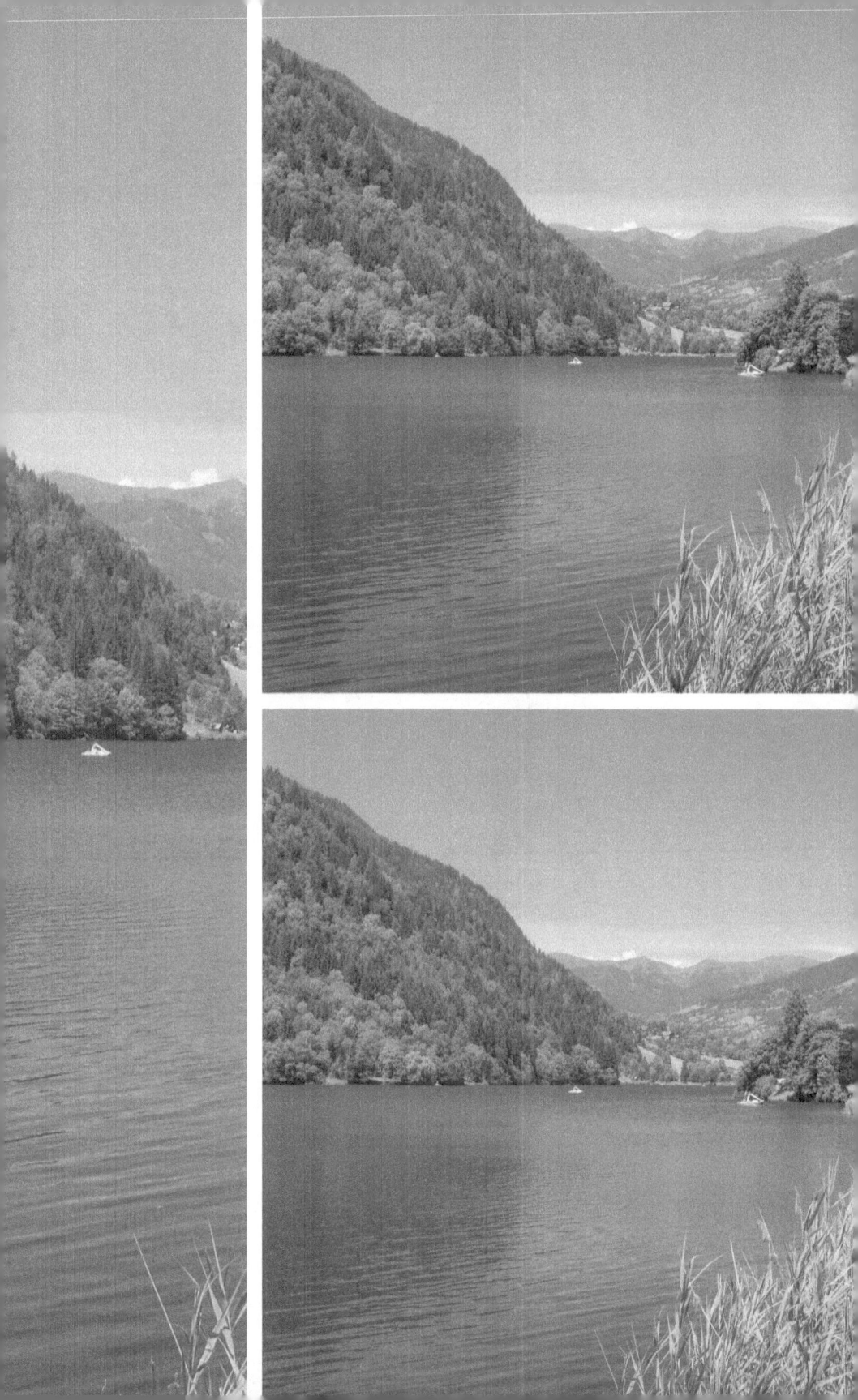

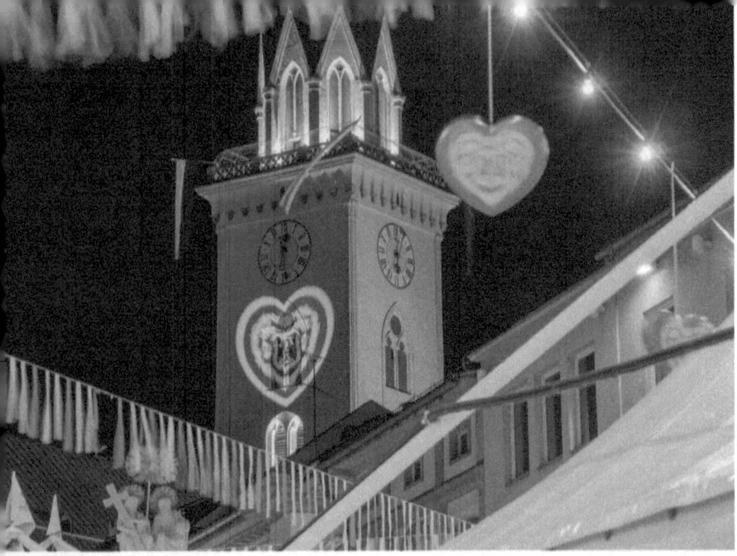

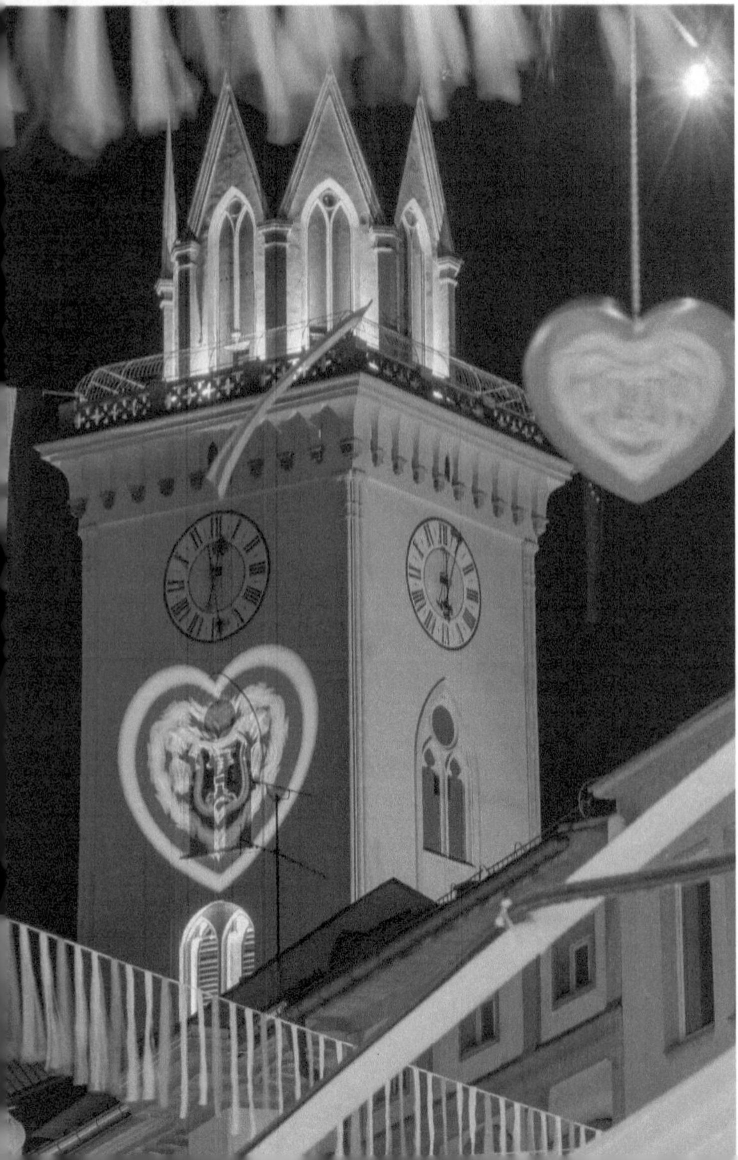

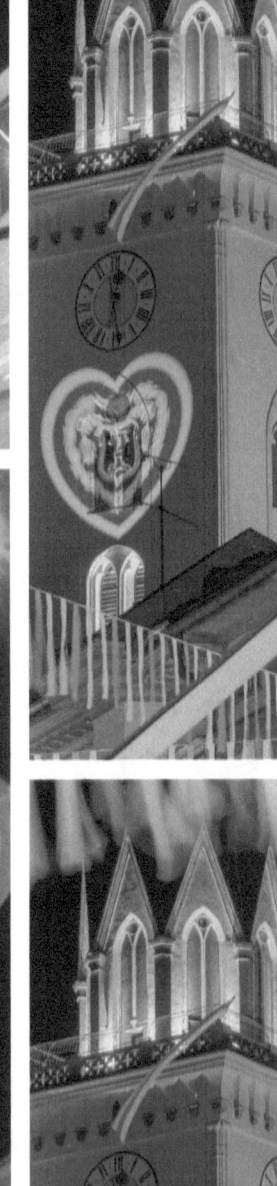
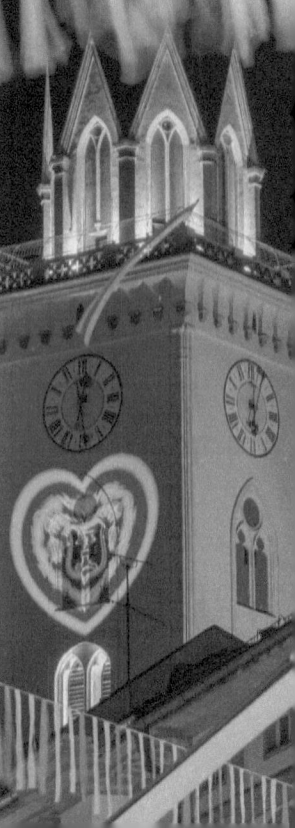

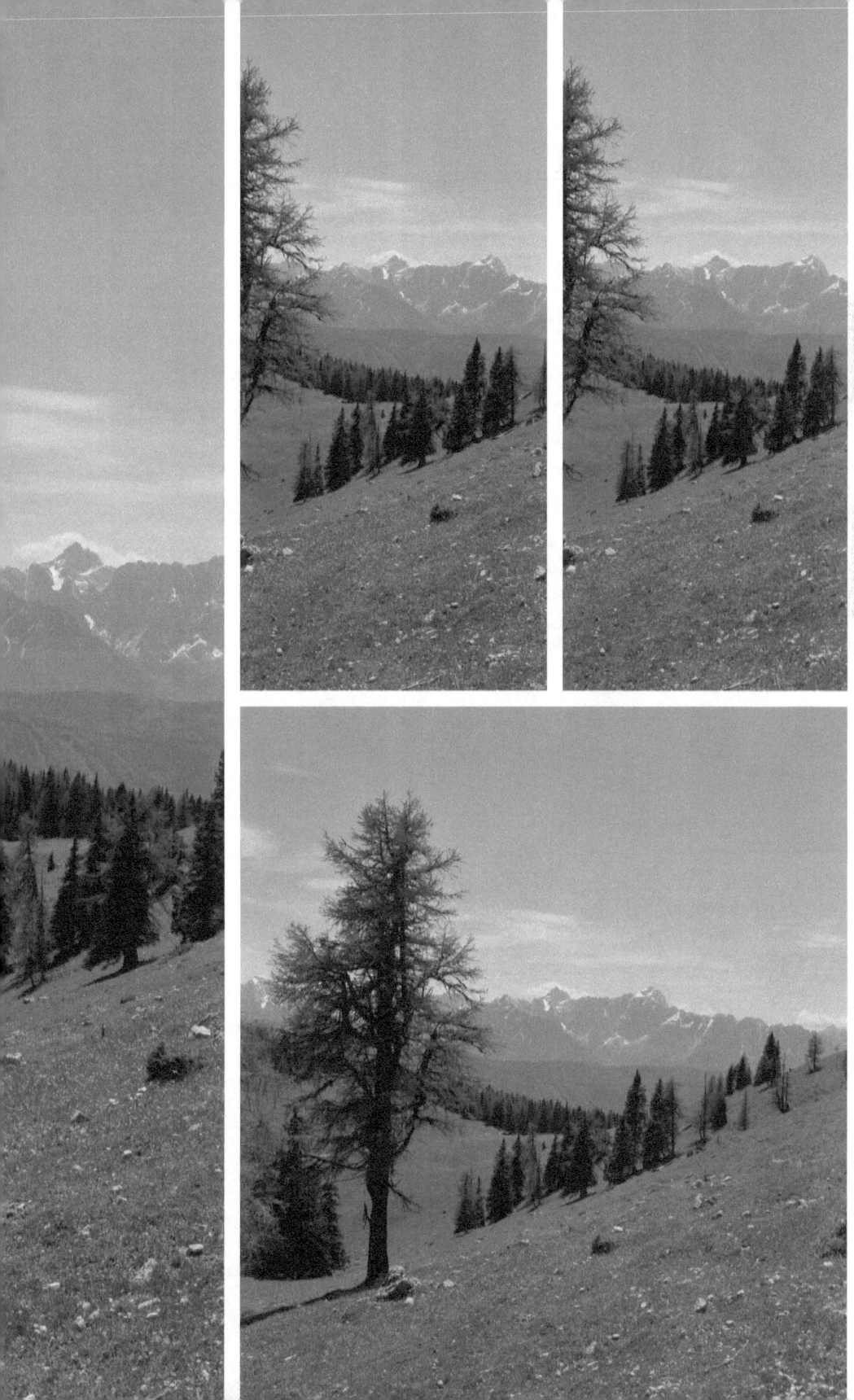

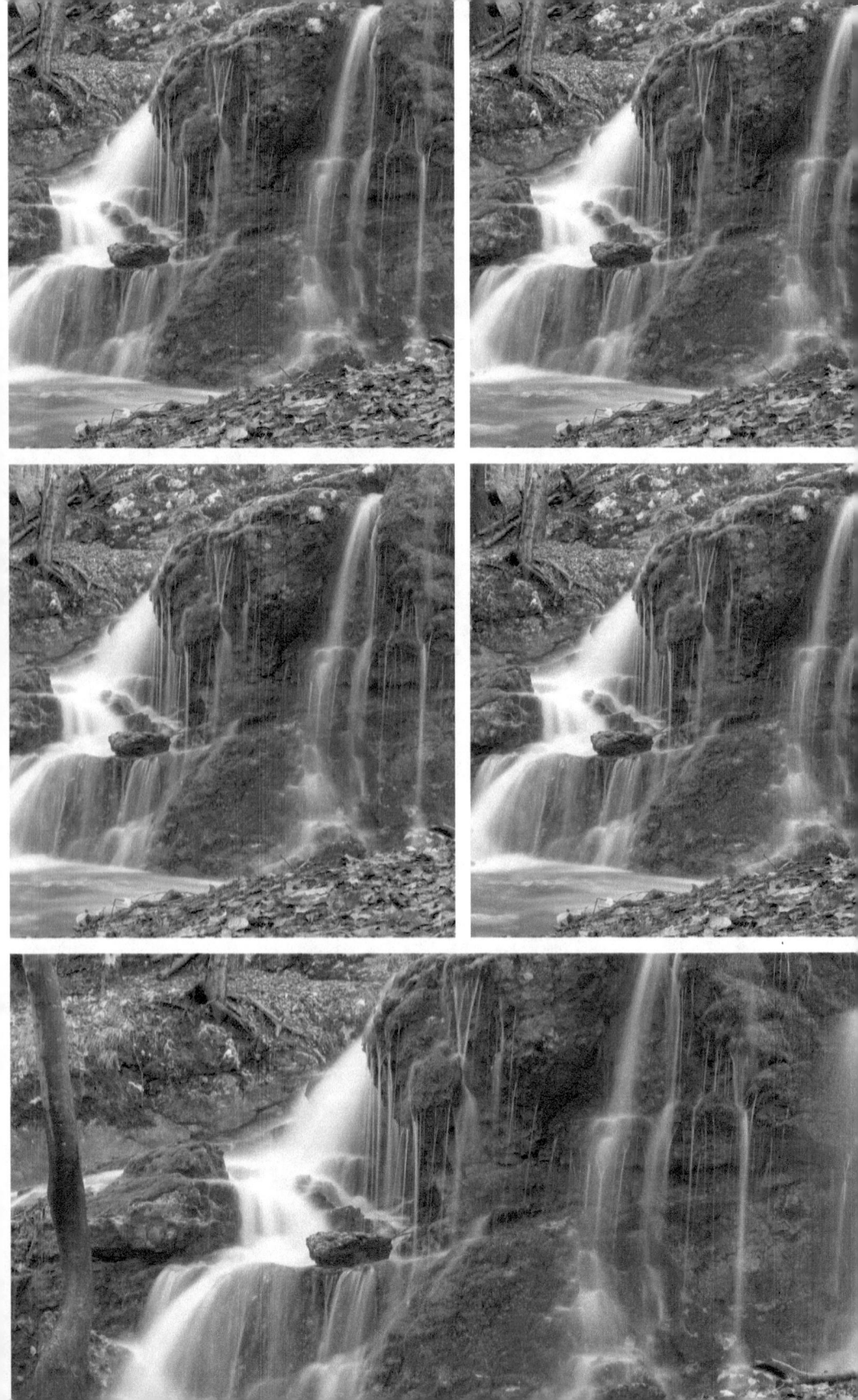

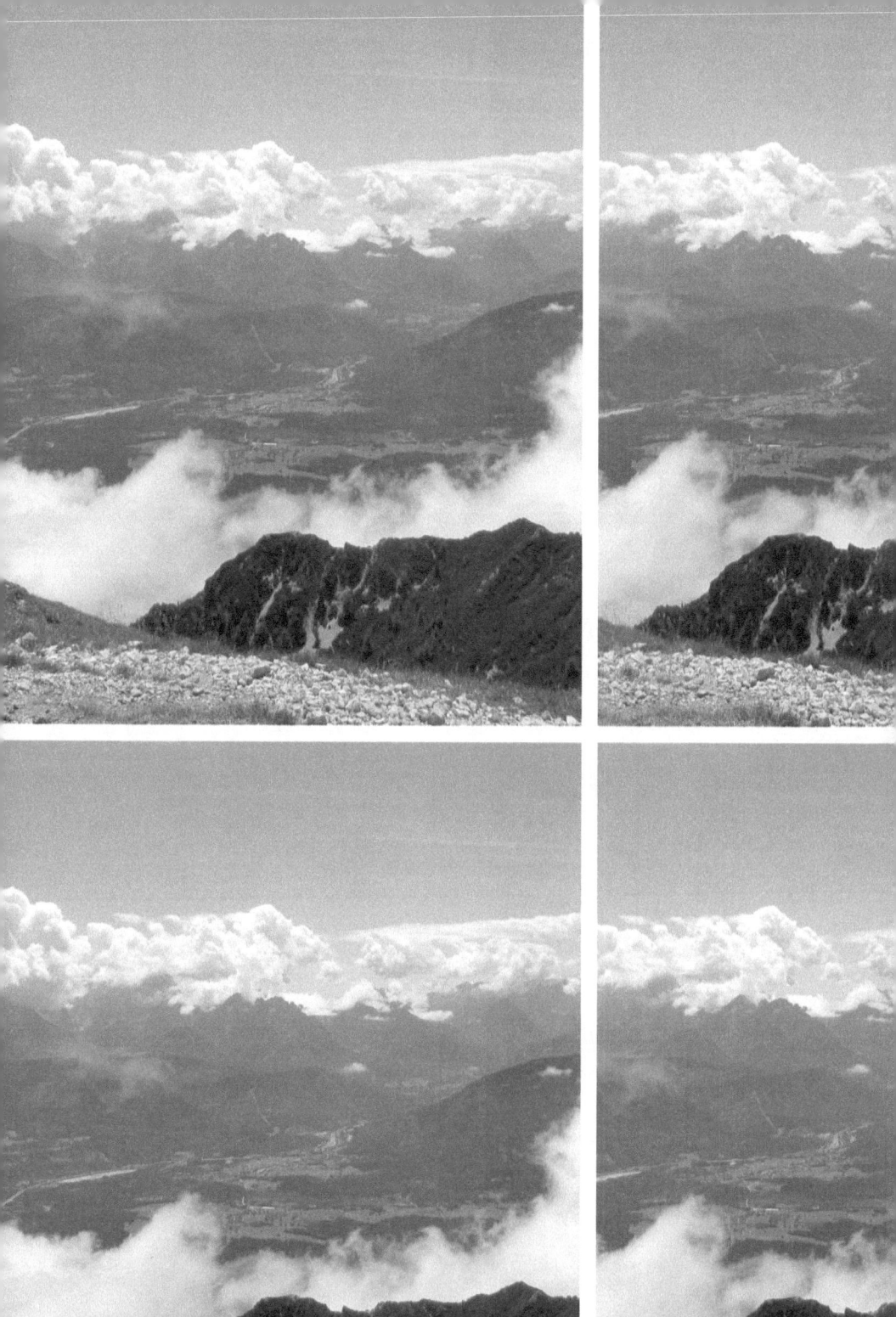

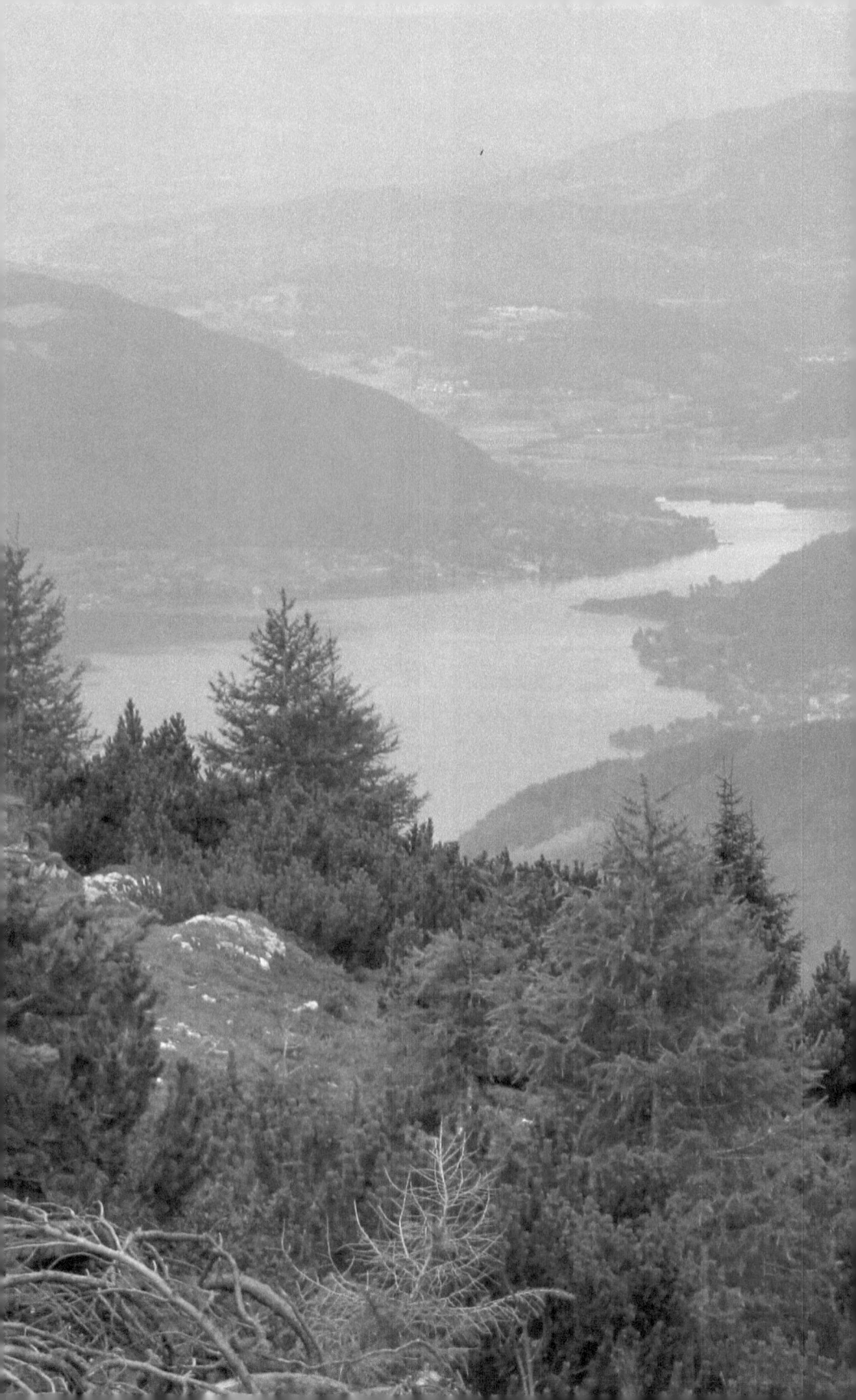

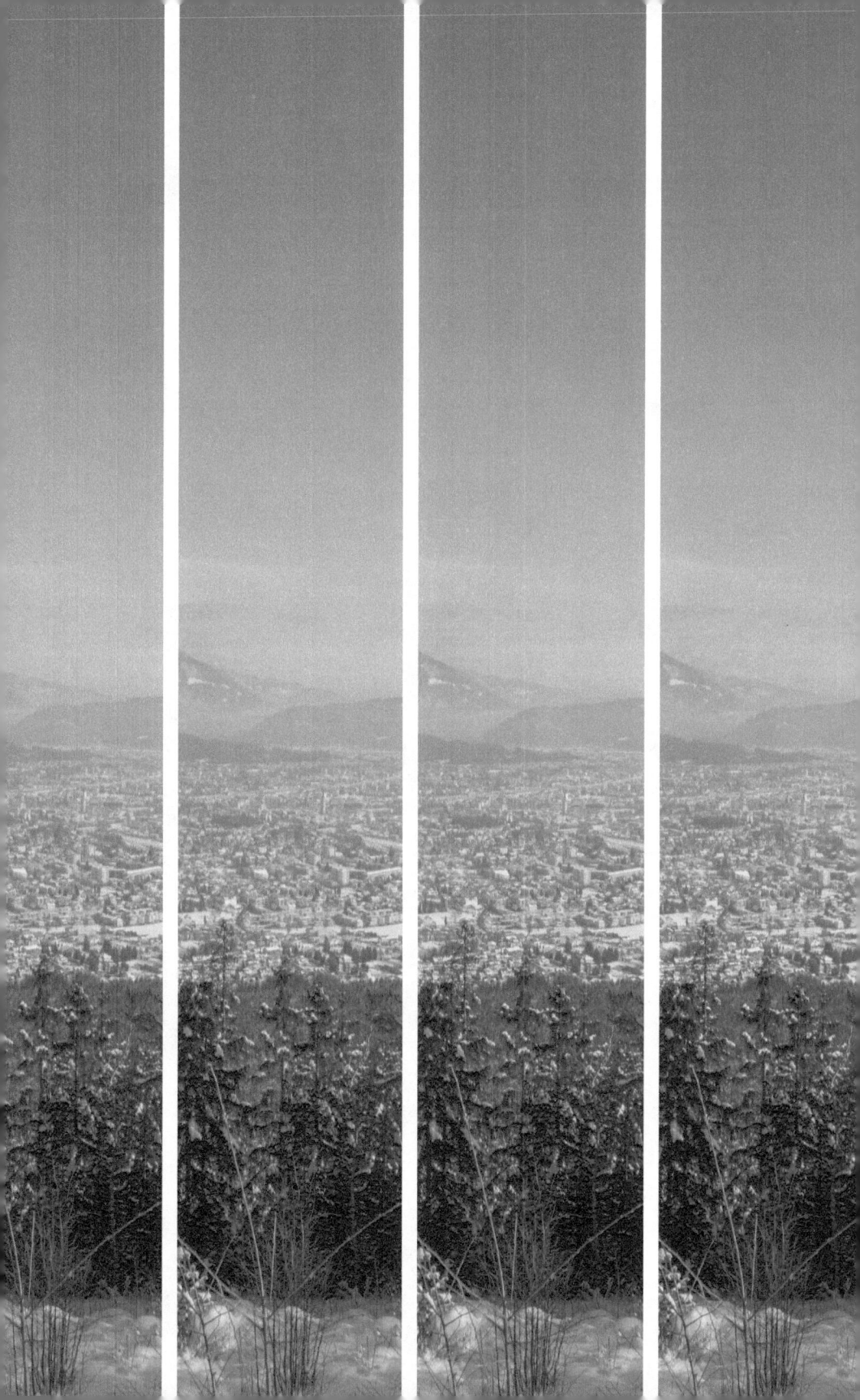

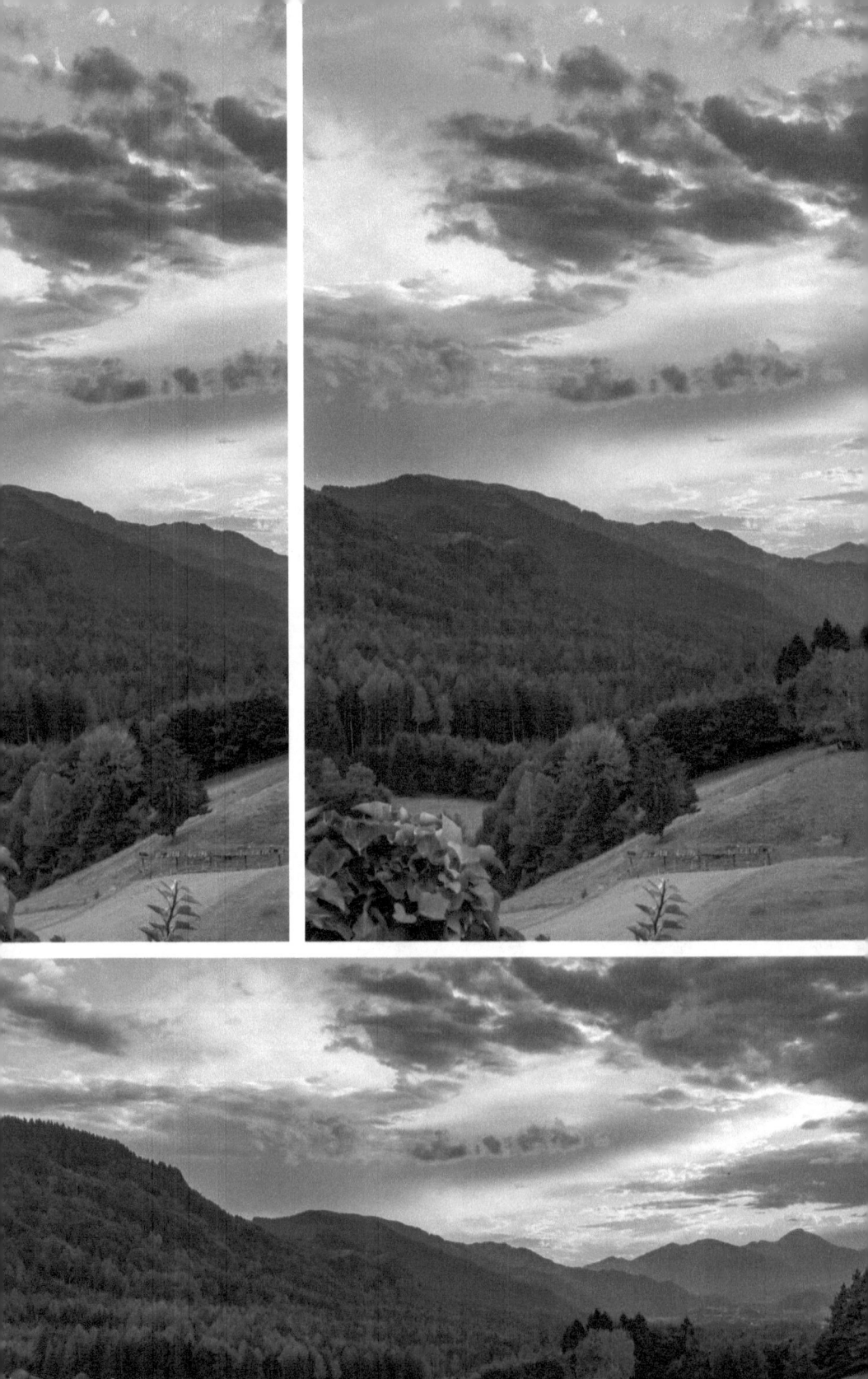

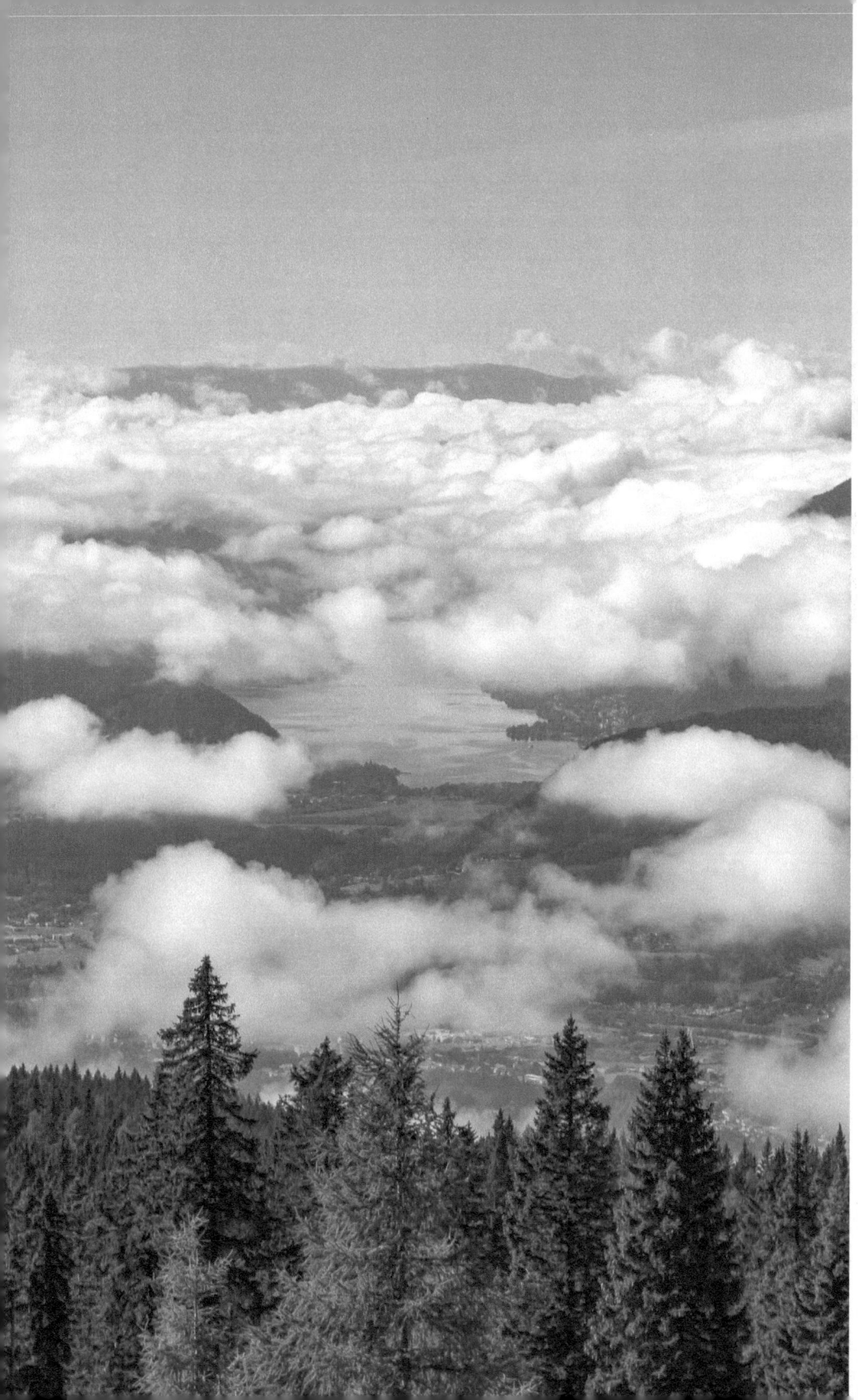

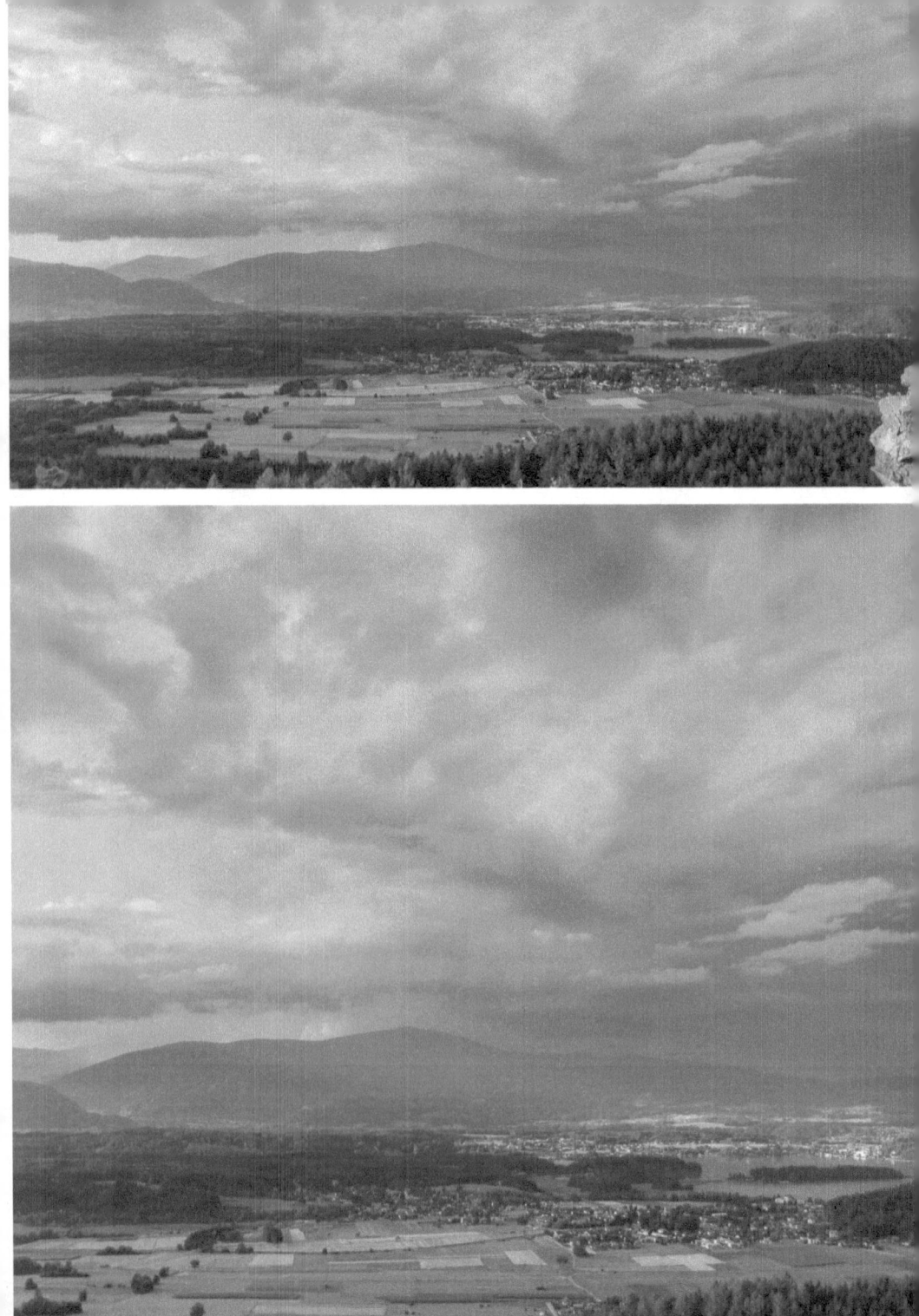

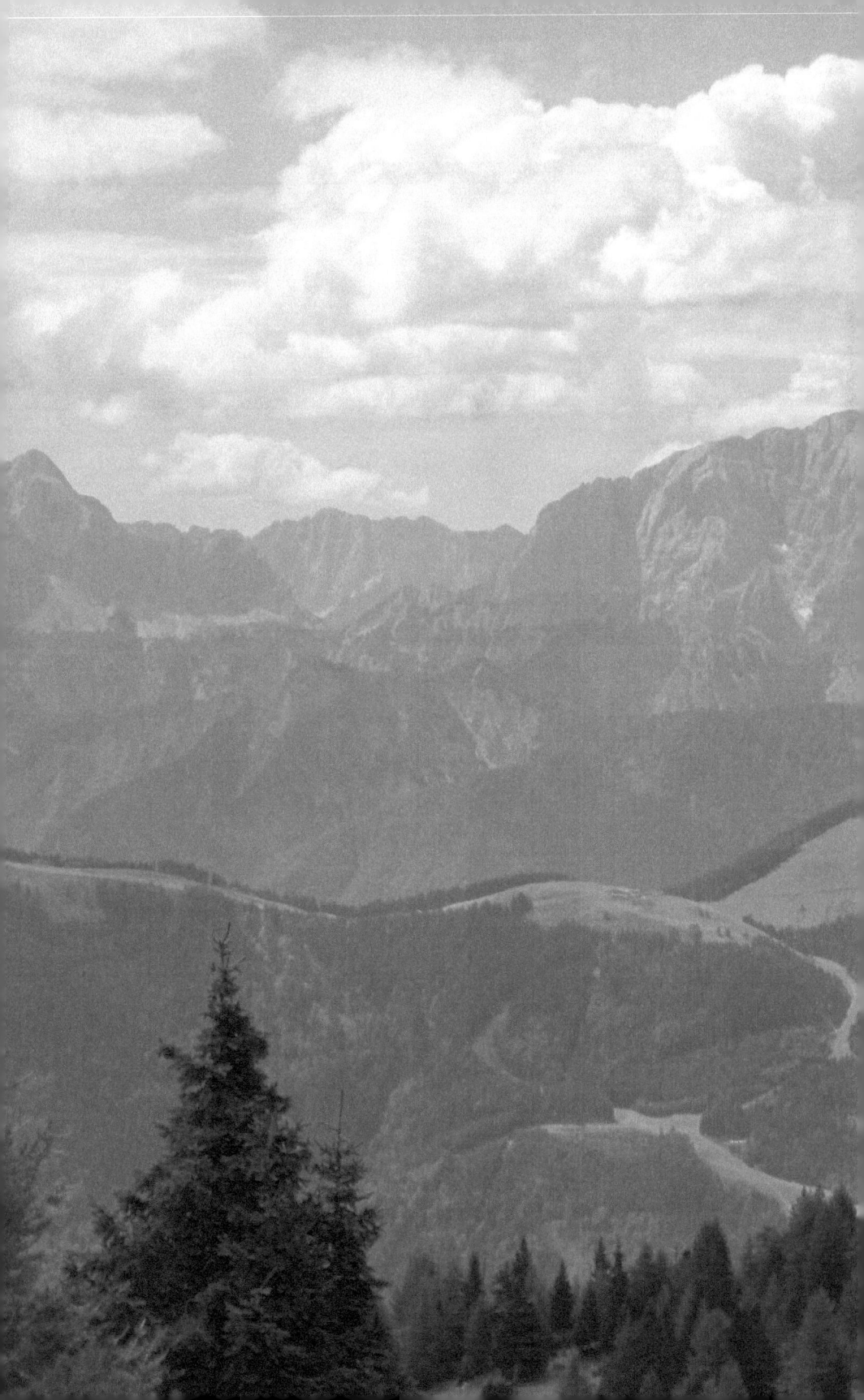

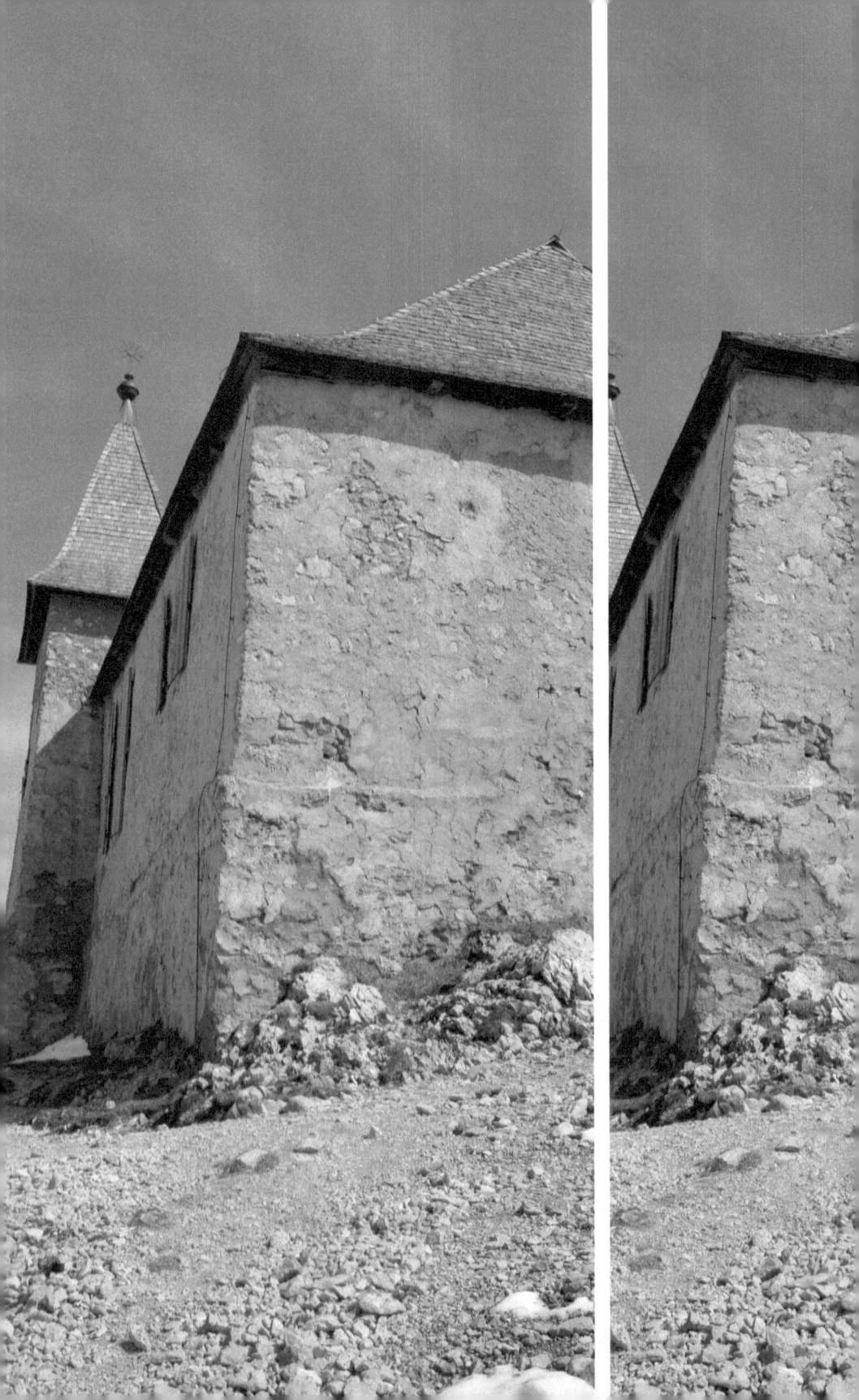

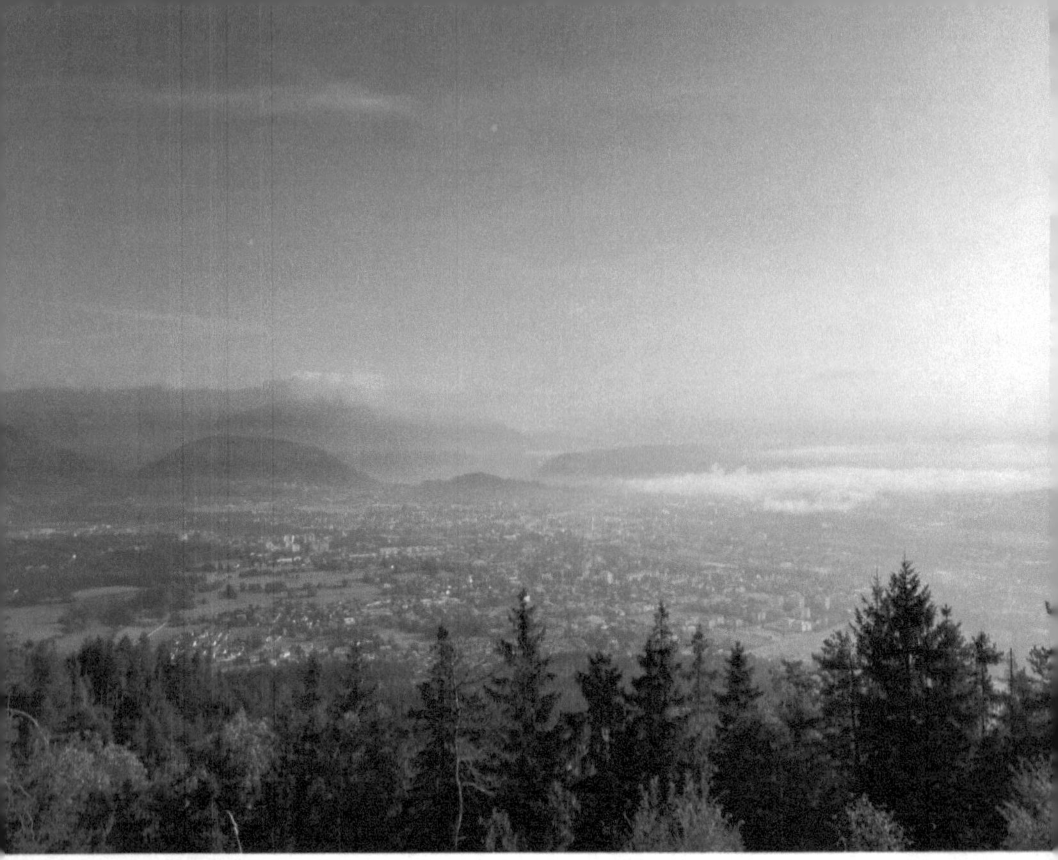

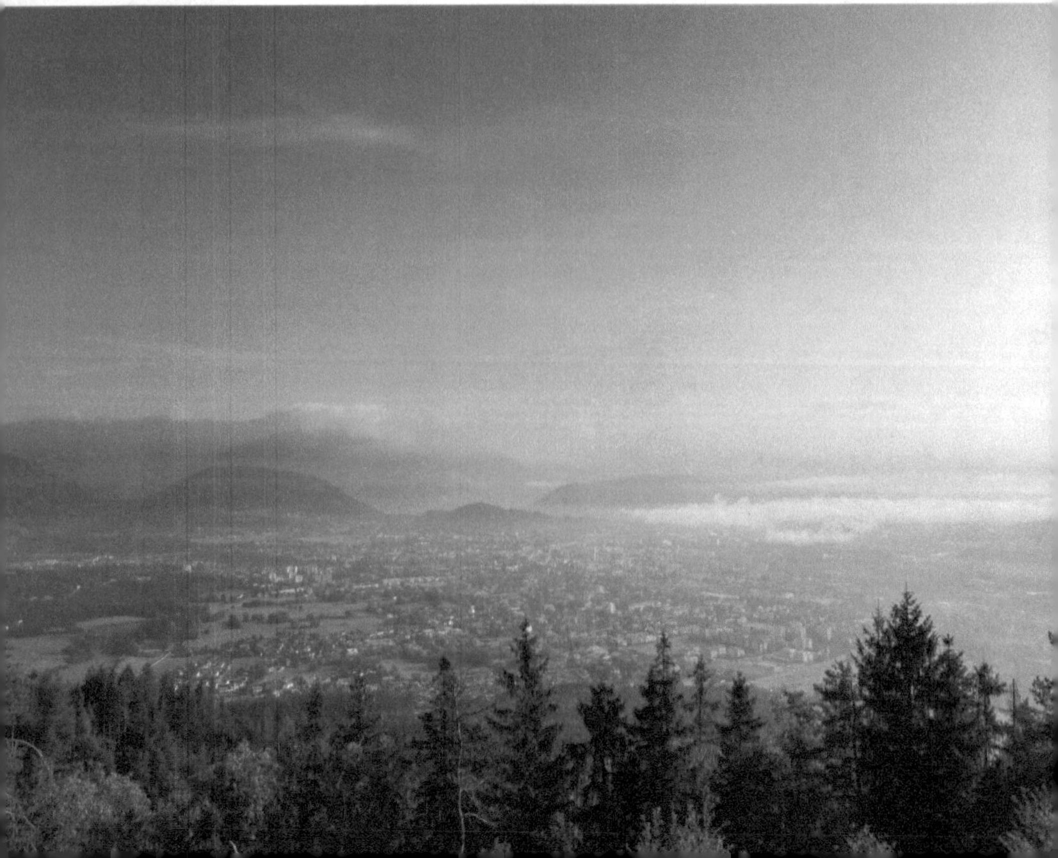

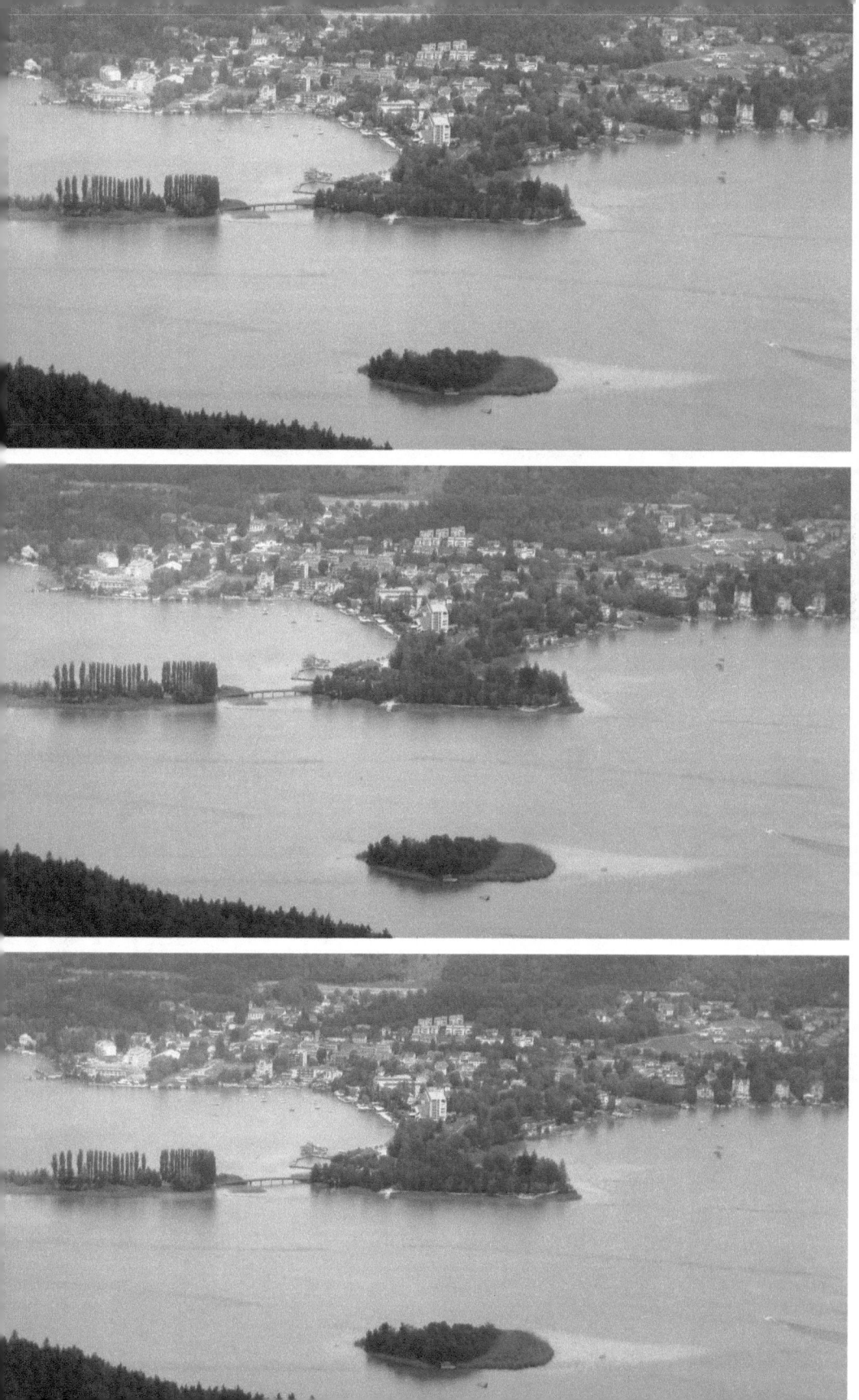

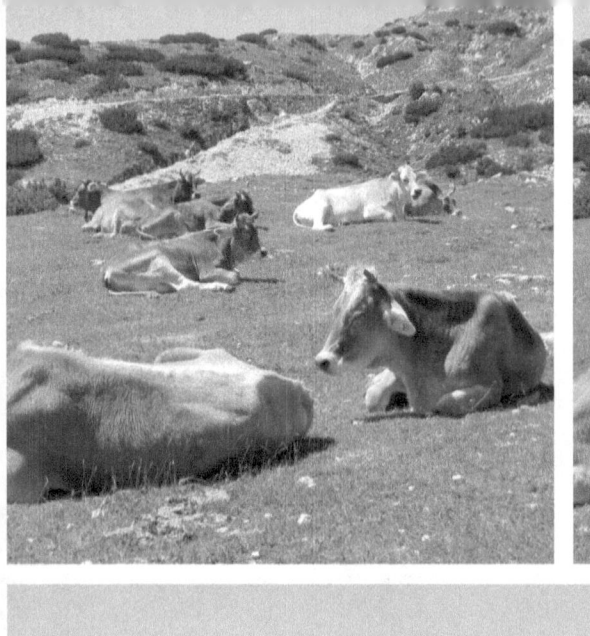
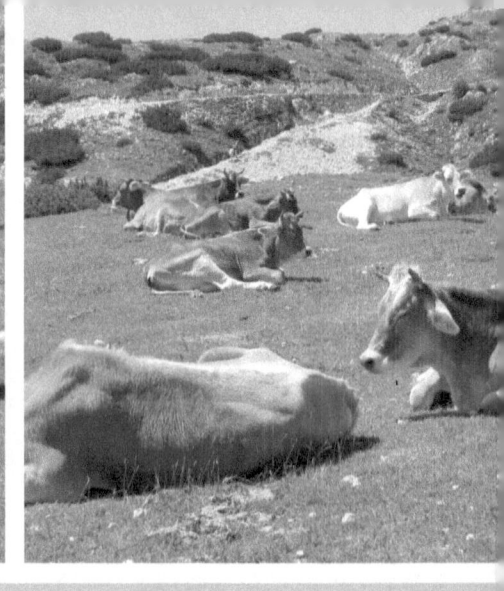

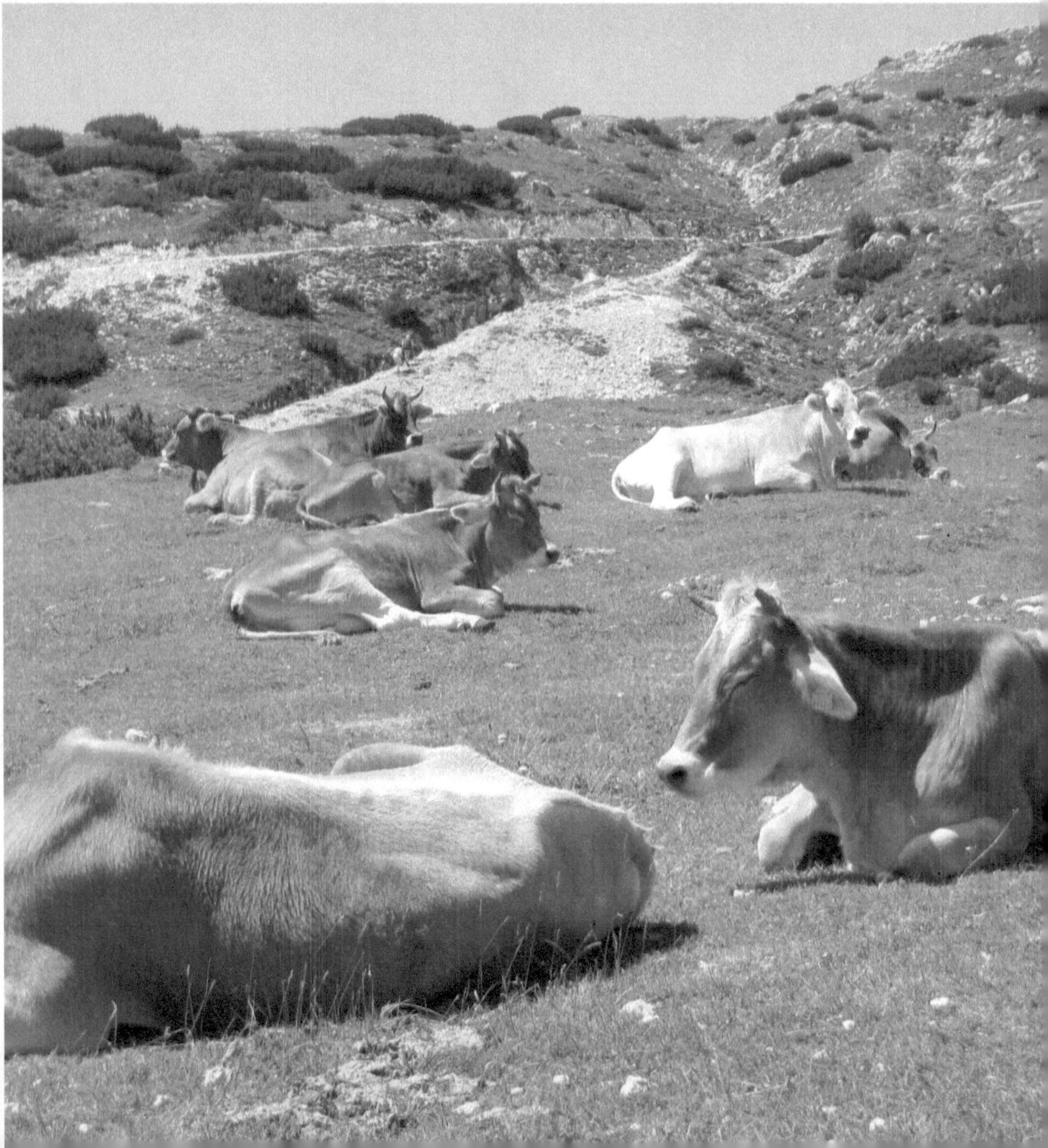

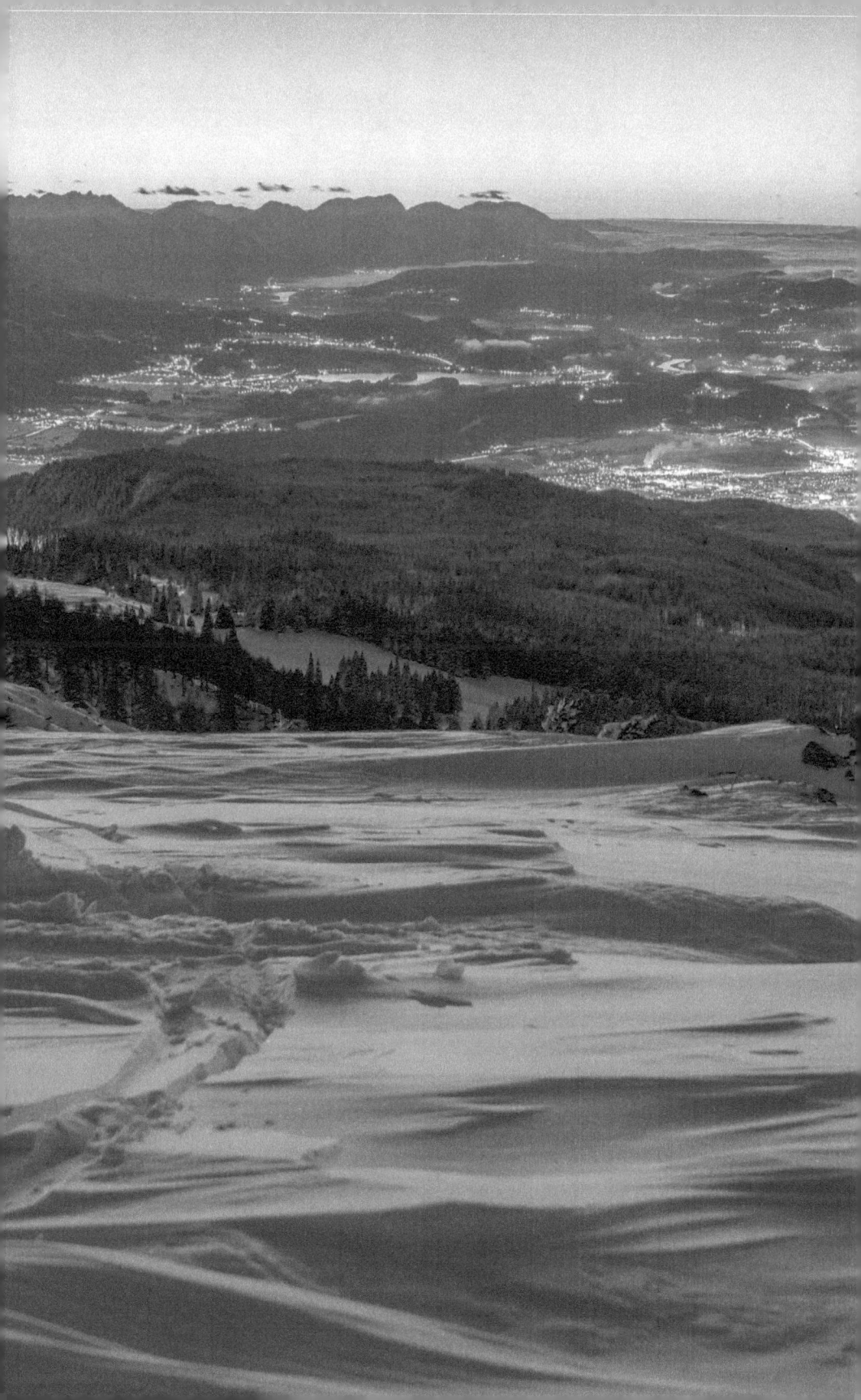

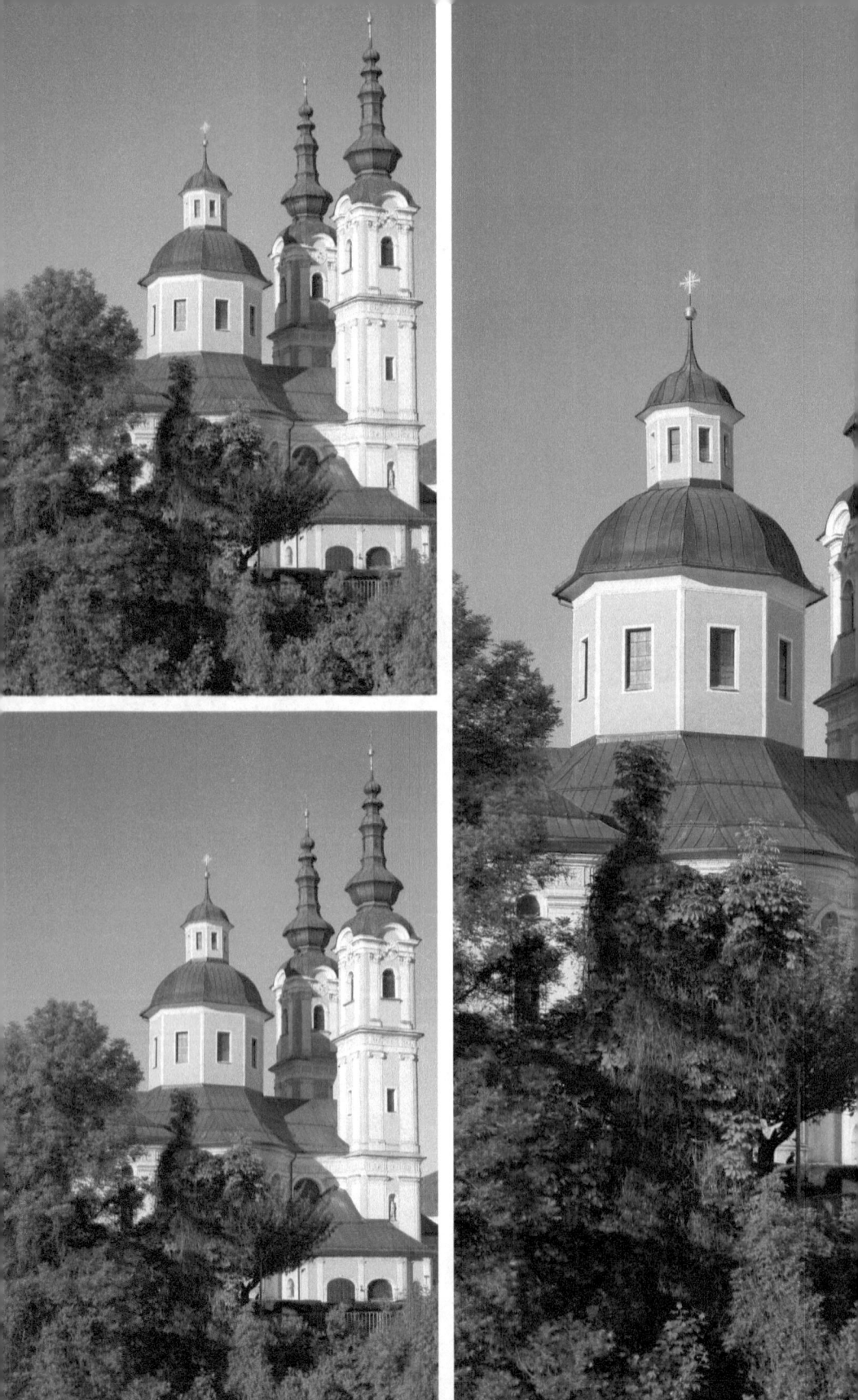

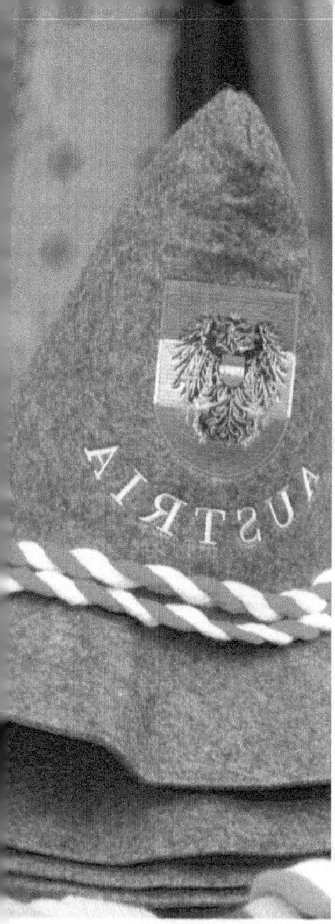
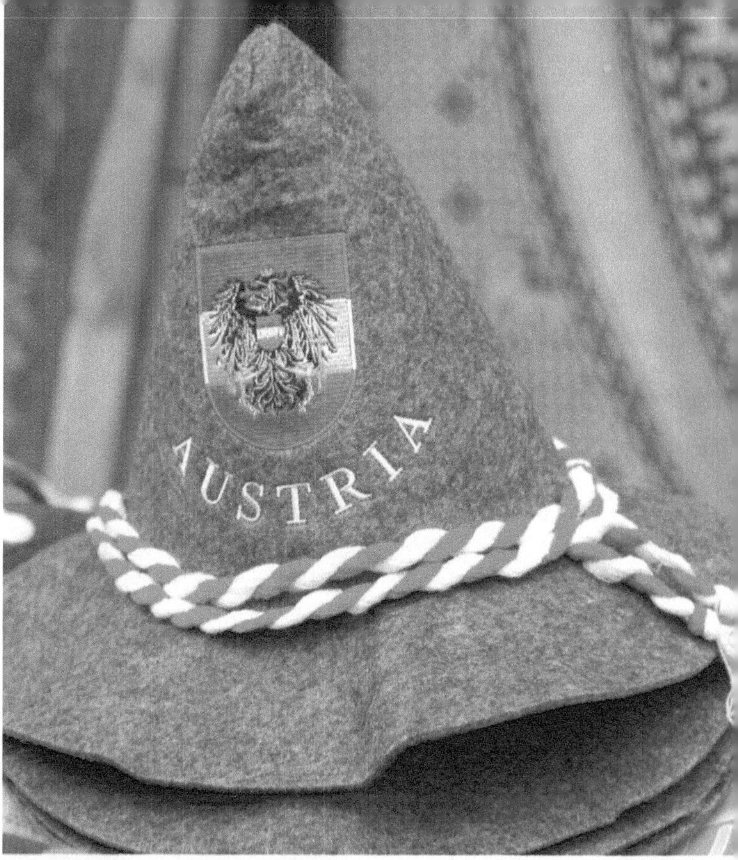
AUSTRIA
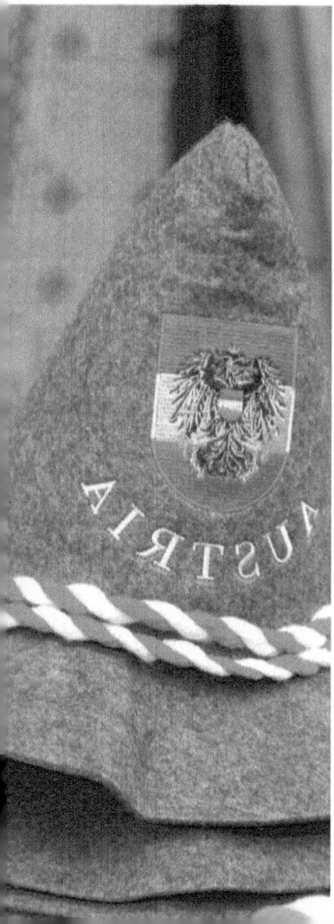
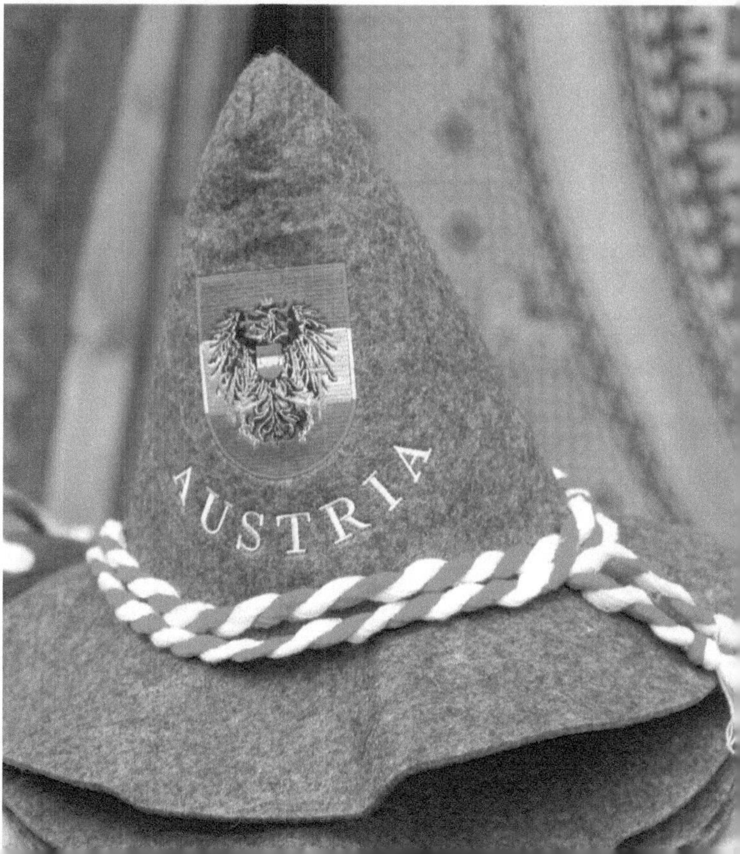
AUSTRIA

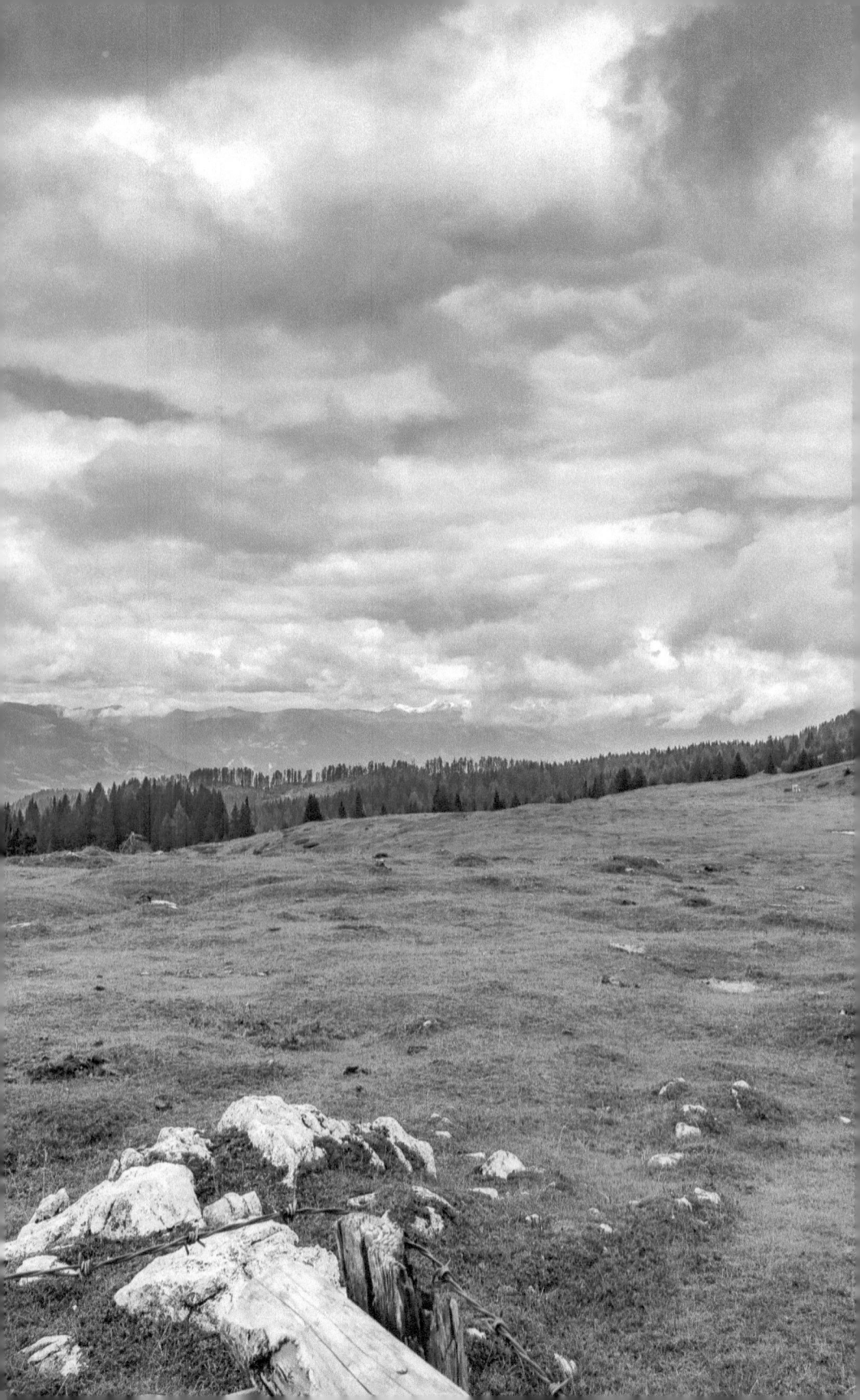

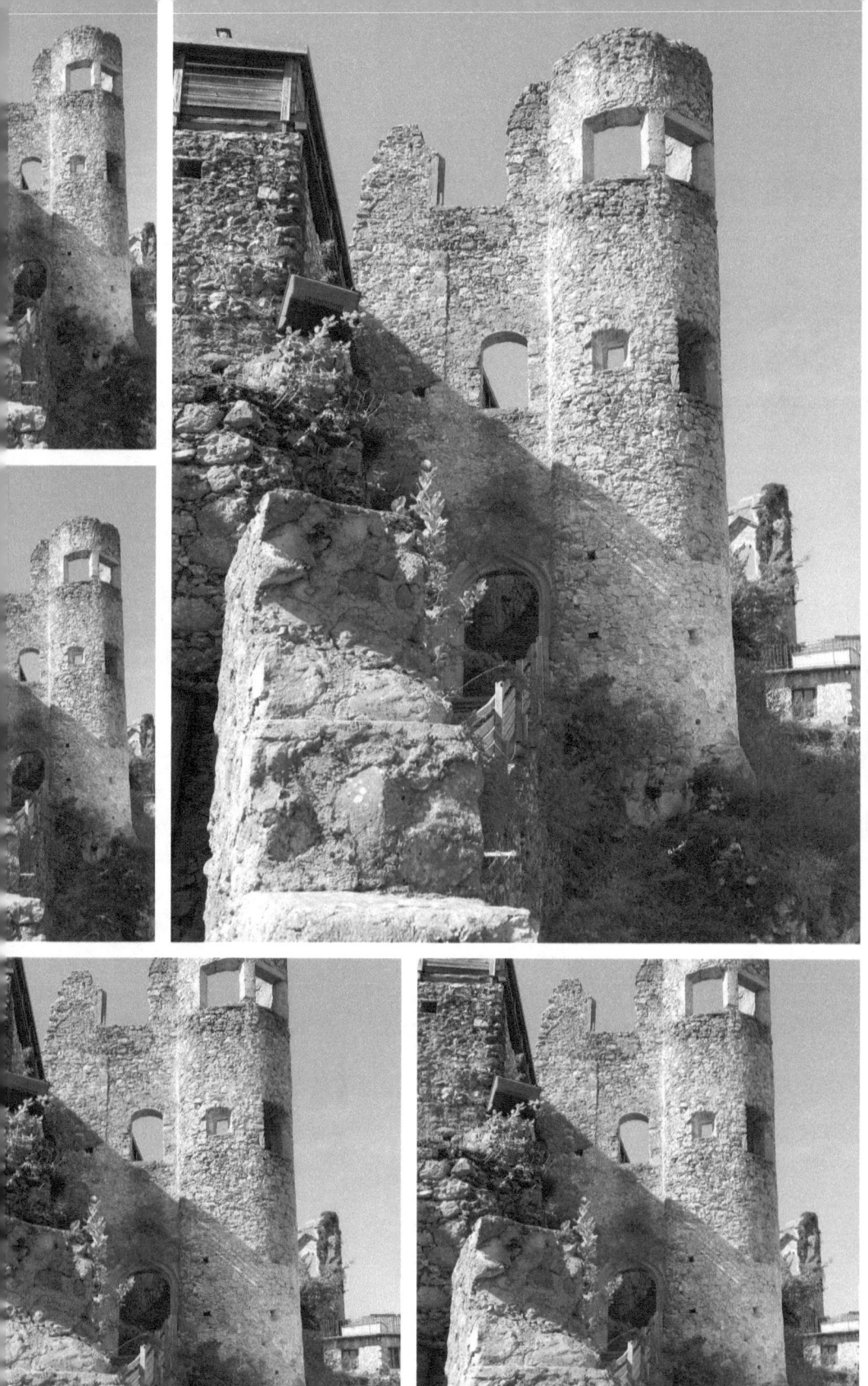

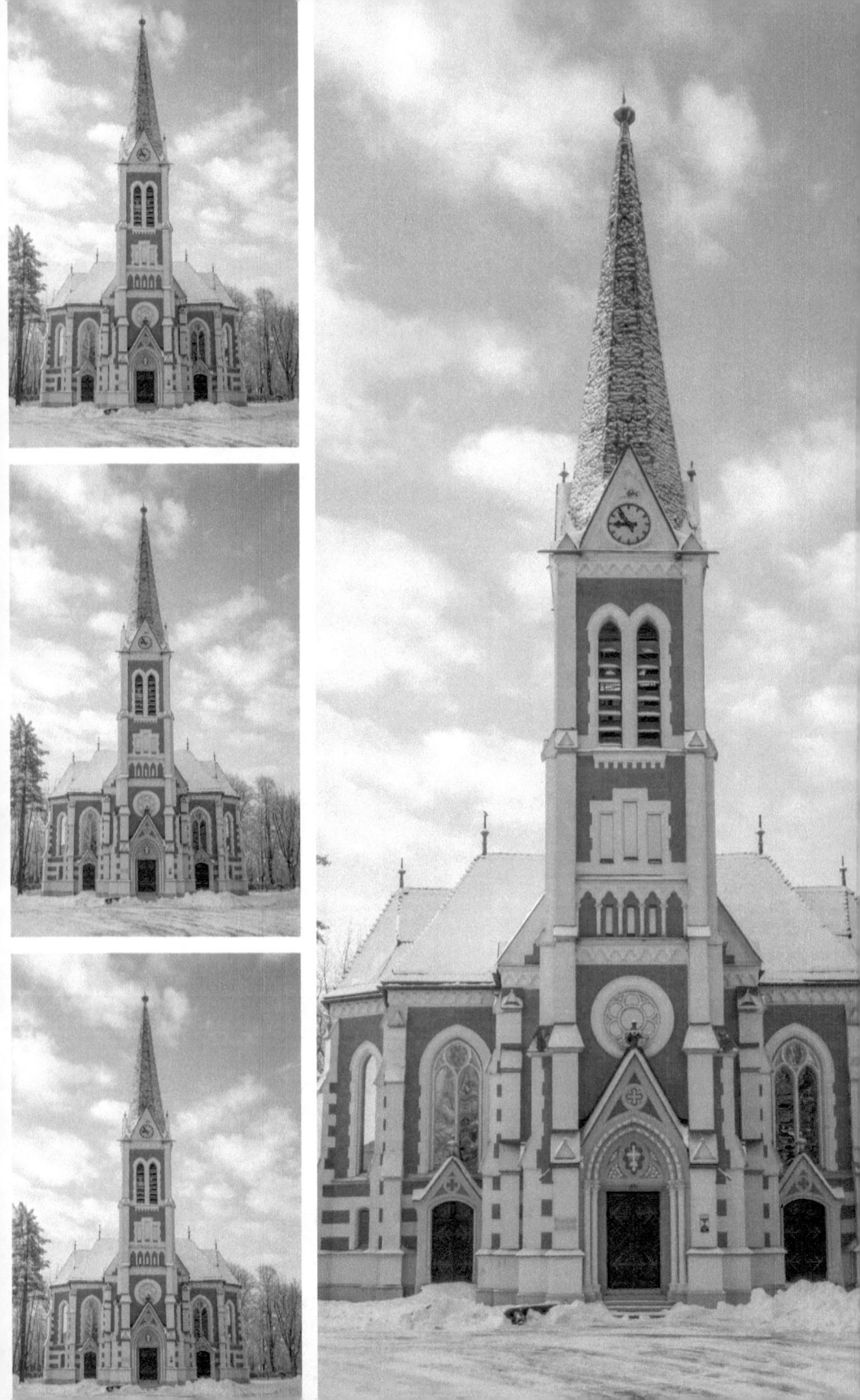

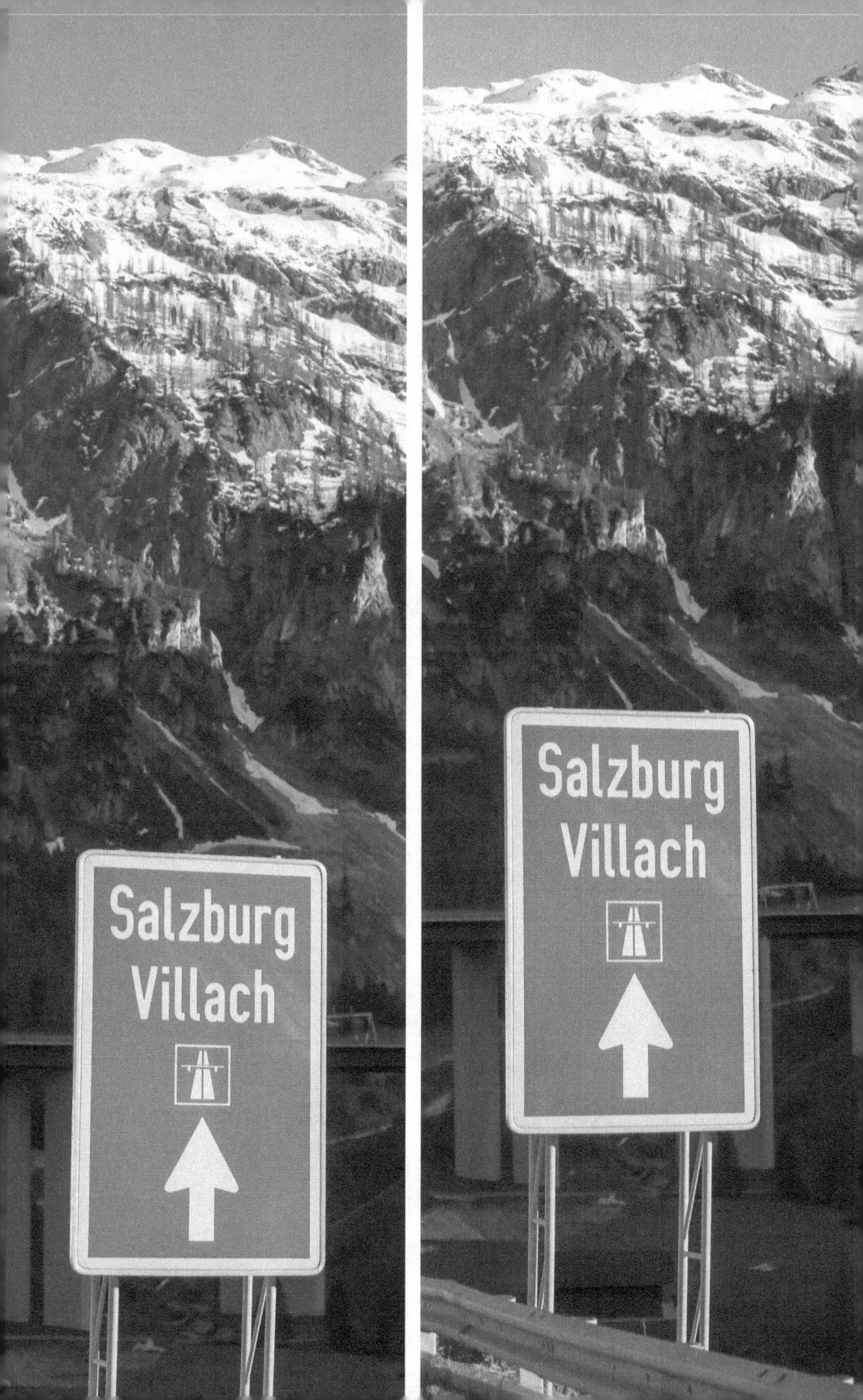

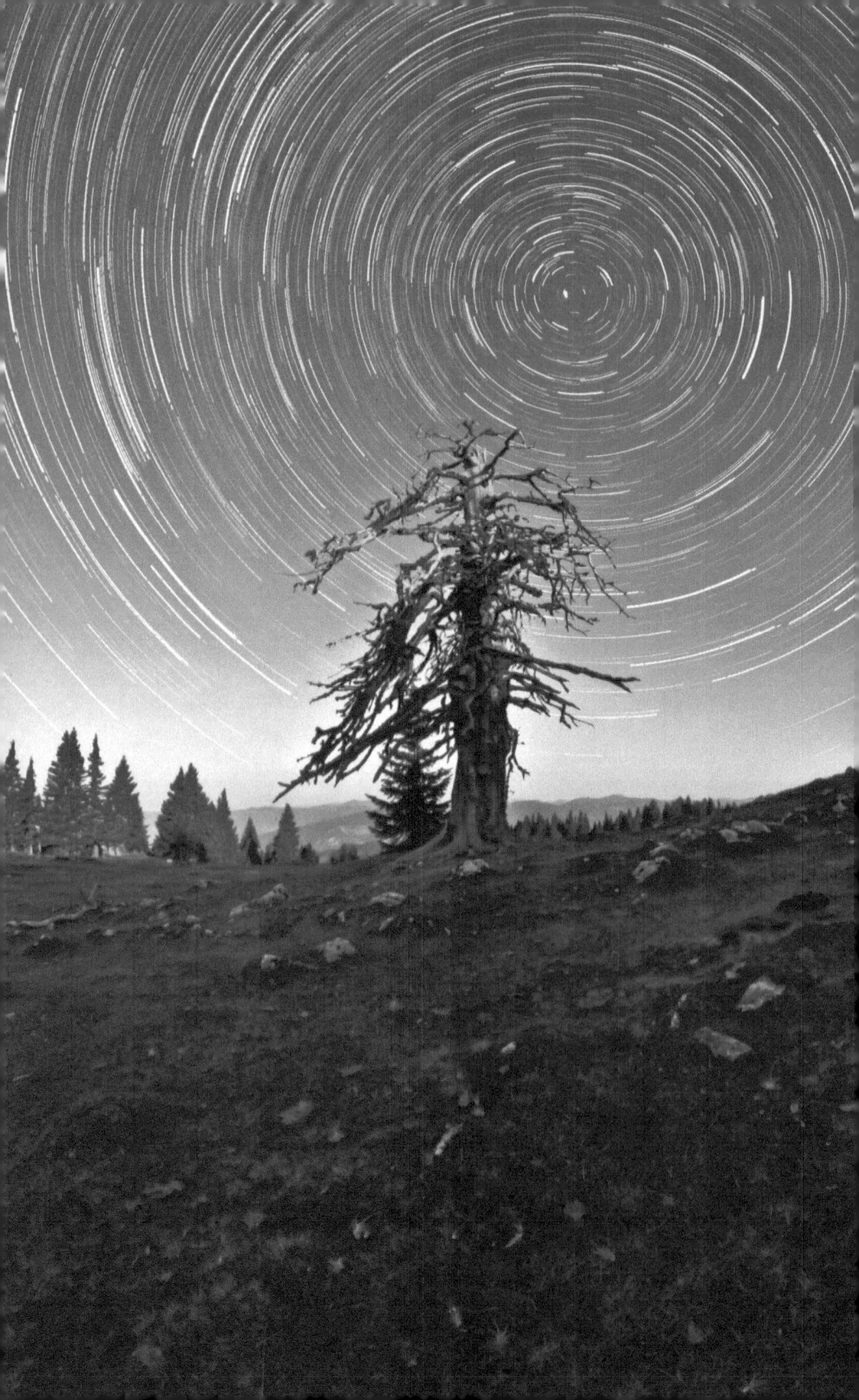

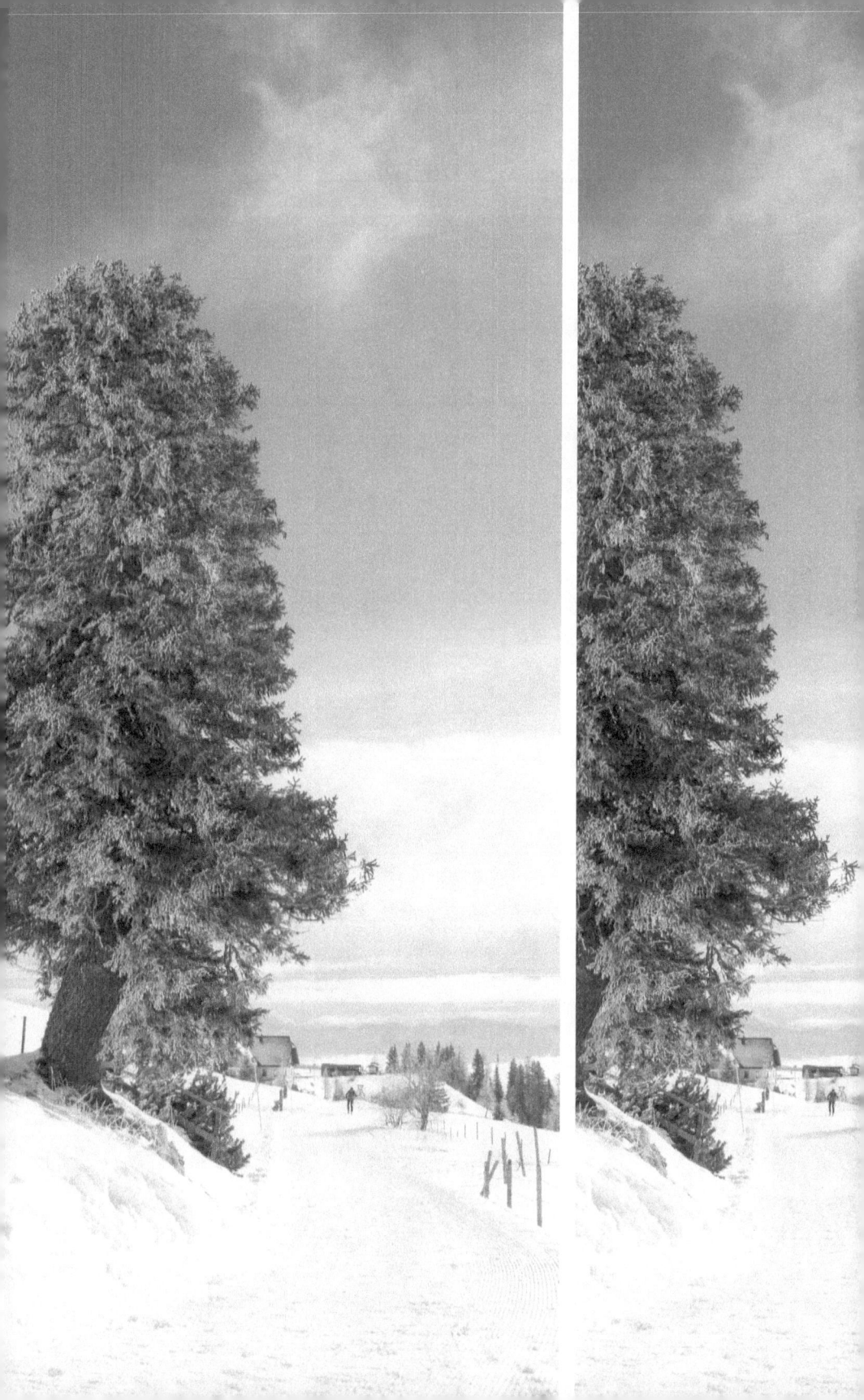

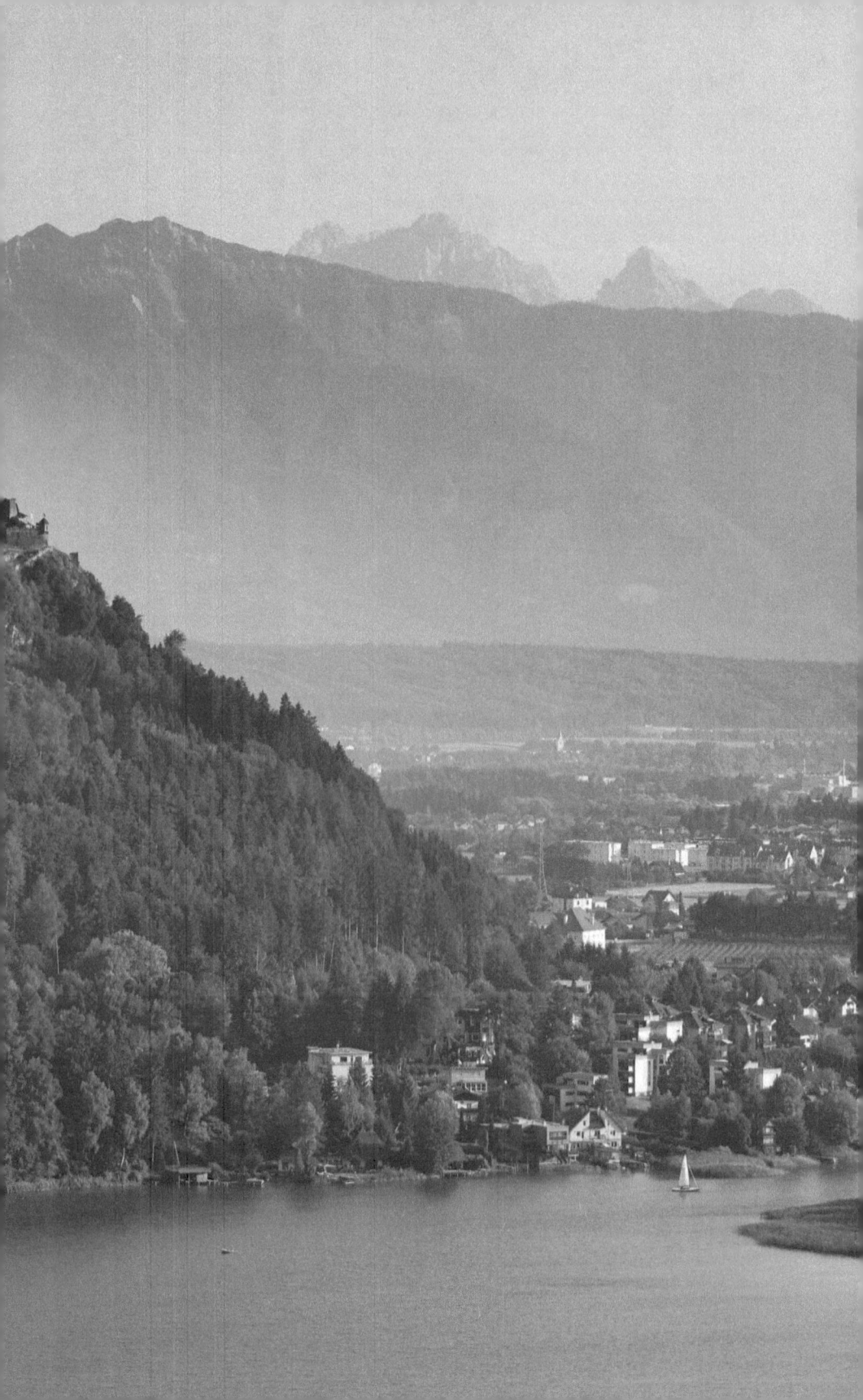

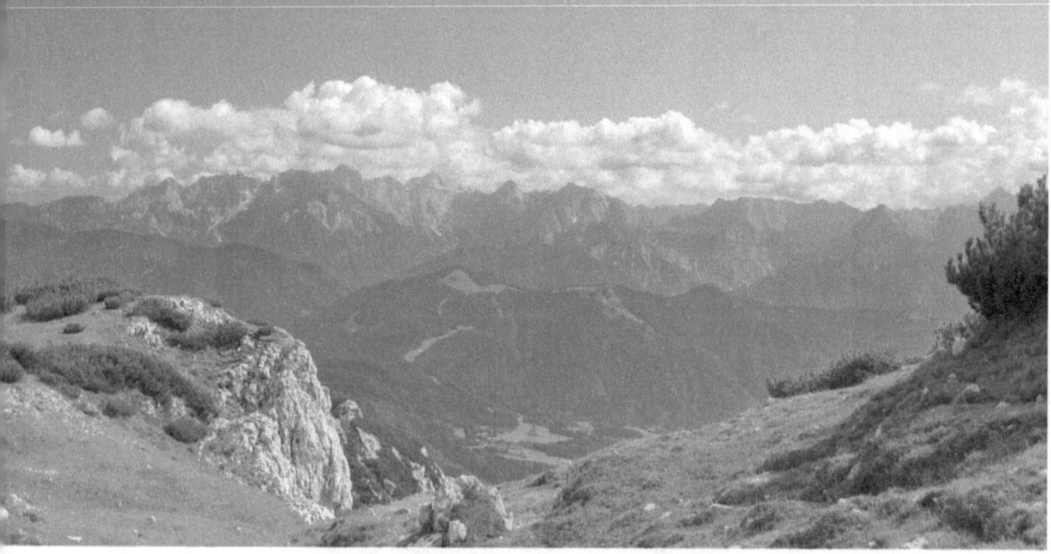

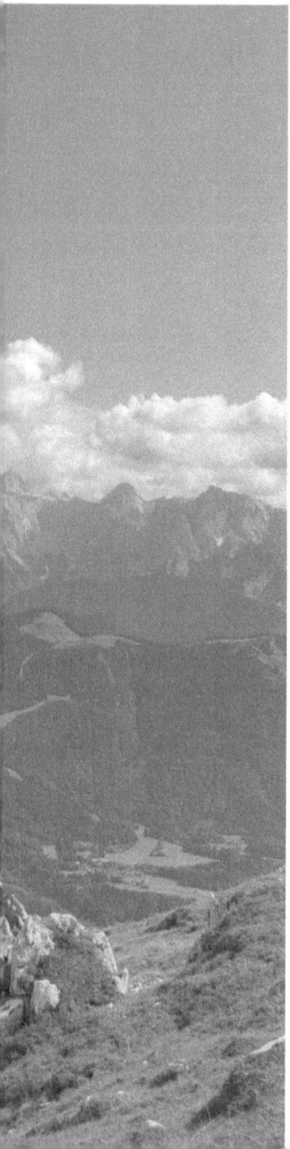

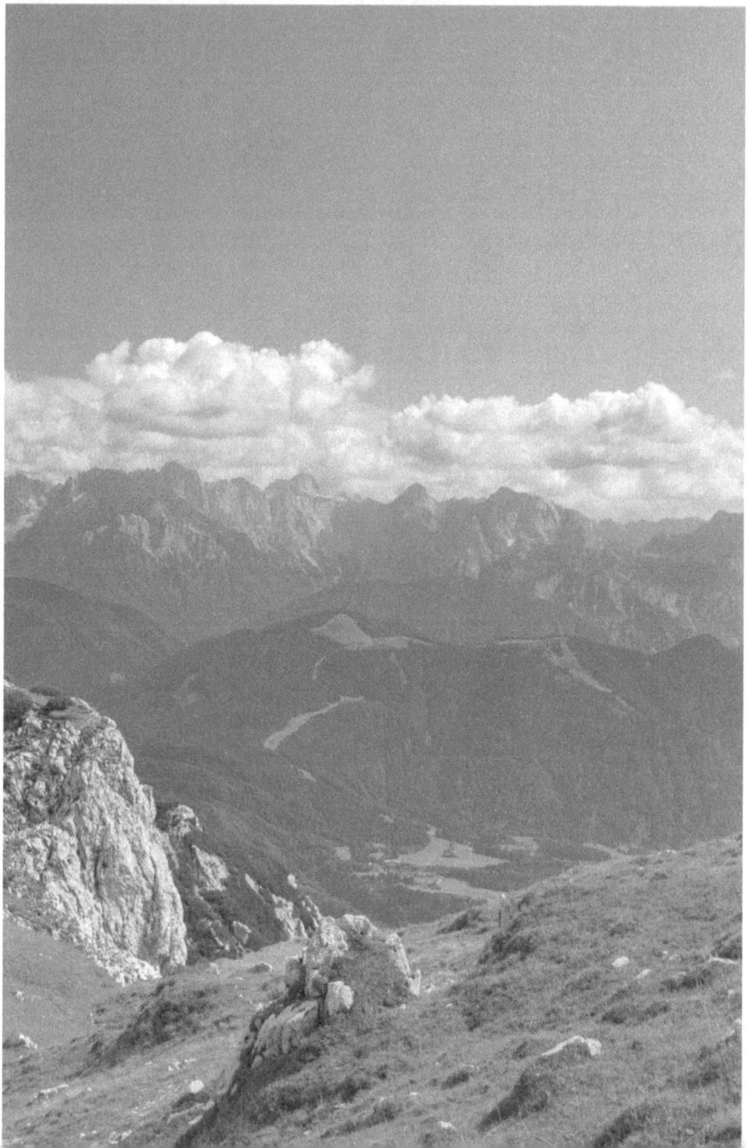

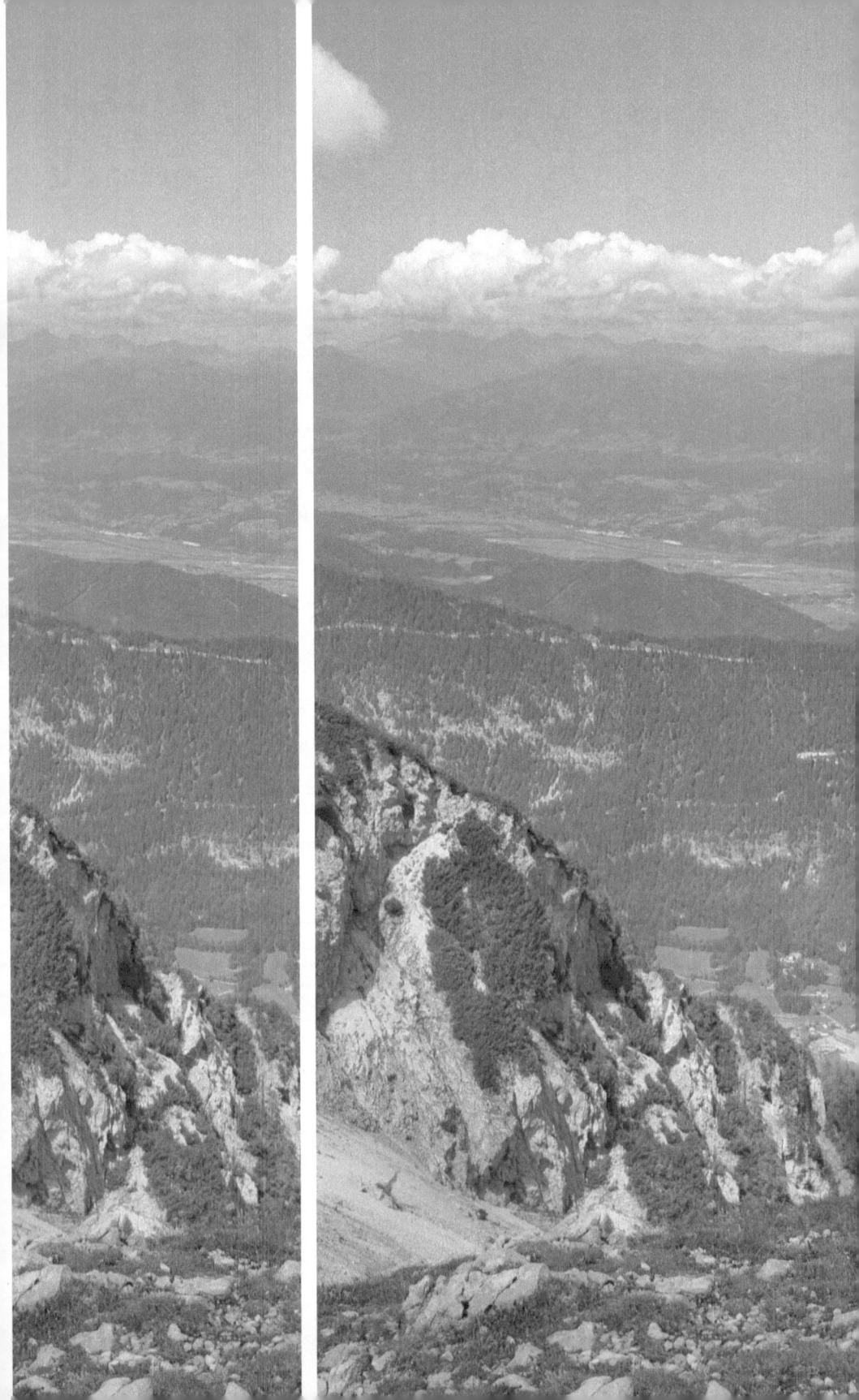

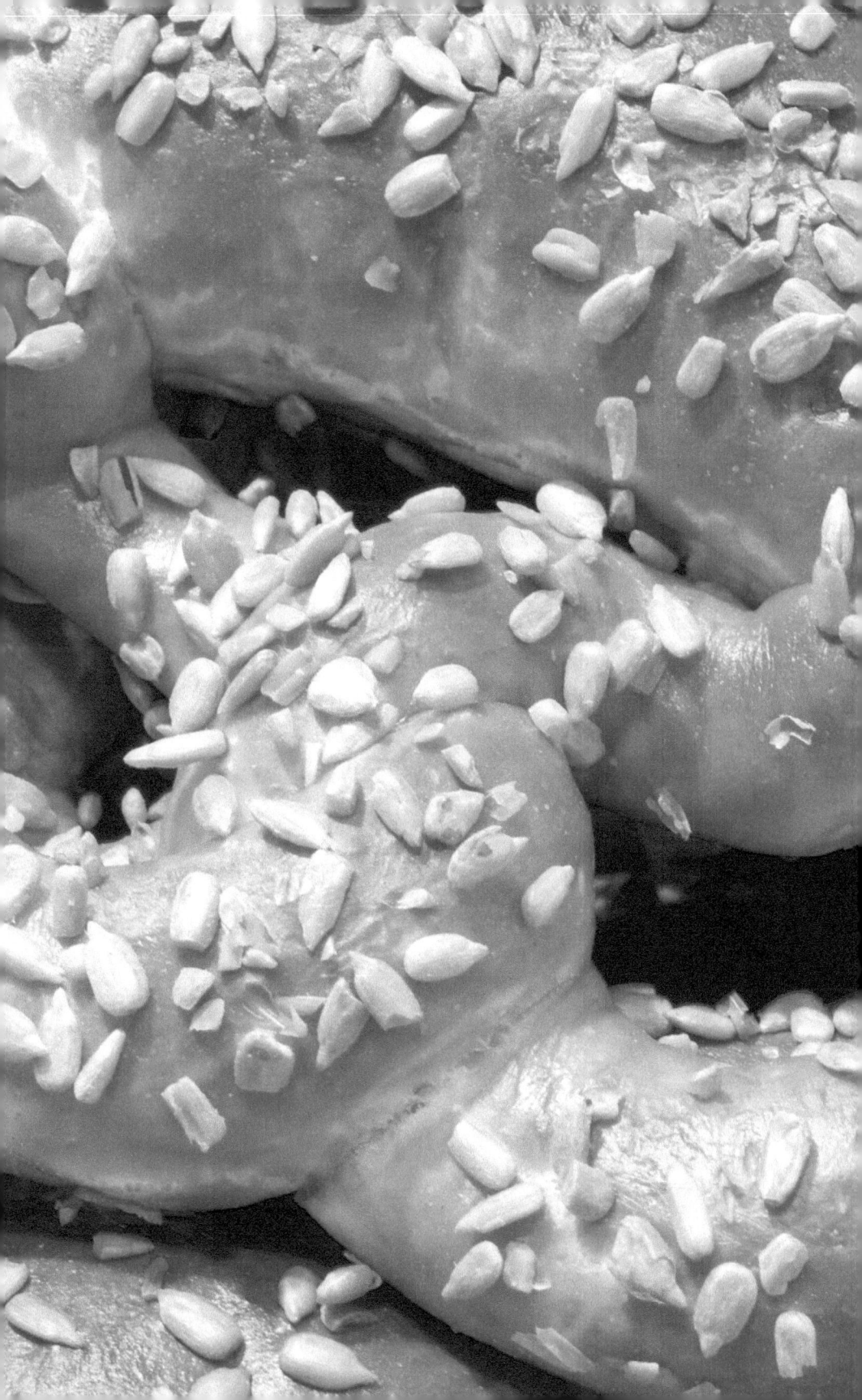

www.ingramcontent.com/pod-product-compliance
Lightning Source LLC
Chambersburg PA
CBHW021023180526

45163CB00005B/2088